Hacking
with
Kali Linux

A Comprehensive Guide for Beginners to Learn Basic Hacking, Cybersecurity, Wireless Networks, and Penetration Testing

By Dylan Mach

Table of Contents

Introduction

Congratulations on purchasing *Hacking with Kali Linux,* and thank you for doing so.

The following chapters will discuss all of the different parts that we need to know more about when it is time to work with the idea of hacking and working with Kali Linux in order to get this all done. There are a lot of different tools that we are able to utilize when it comes to hacking, but one of the very best operating systems that we are able to use to make this into a reality is the Kali Linux system. This guidebook is going to take some time to go through all of that and learn more about how we can make it all work.

The start of this guidebook is going to take a look at some of the basics of hacking, the reasons that we would want to spend some time looking at hacking and using it for our own networks, and a good look at the difference between ethical hackers, unethical hackers, and everyone in between.

From there, we are going to take a look at a bit about cybersecurity and cyber attacks. With our modern world and the fact that so many people are online and trying to share and look at information all of the time, it is no wonder that hackers are trying to find methods that will allow them to get onto the computers and networks out there to steal personal and financial information any time that they would like. That is why we are going to take some time to look at how we can keep our networks safe and secure with cybersecurity while also knowing which types of cyber attacks are the most likely.

Now it is time to take this a bit further and look more at how hacking is going to work. We are going to take a look at the hacking process in more details, while also looking at malware, and how that, and a few other types of attacks are going to be able to come into play to help us really see results.

Then it is time to move on to some of the things that we are able to do with the Kali Linux system. This is often considered one of the best coding operating systems to work with, and we are going to take the time to look at what it is about and how we are able to use it for our needs. In this part, we are going to look at the reasons that people like to work with Linux, how to set up Kali Linux, how to work with Kali in a Virtual Machine if this is the best option for us, and even how to organize Kali Linux, so it is ready for some of the attacks that we want to do.

This is just the beginning of what we are able to do when it comes to hacking. Now that we have set the stage and we are all ready to go with some of this, it is time to take it a bit further and look at some of the neat things that we can use

Kali Linux to help us out with. We are going to look at how to scan and manage our networks, the importance of firewalls, how to obtain user information when we want, the use of Kali Linux on some of the portable devices we want to use, and even how to work with MalDuino and Kismet.

This is not all, though. We are going to take a look at a few more of the steps that we are able to work with when it is time to hack a network of our choice and gather up the information that we would like. To finish out this guidebook, we are also going to spend some time looking at how we are able to bypass a hidden SSHS, how to hack onto the WPA and WPA2 wireless systems, how to use some of the different tools out there to make sure that you stay hidden and no one will be able to trace the attacks back to you, and how we are able to use Metasploit to help us complete our own penetration testing.

As we can see with this guidebook, there are a ton of different parts that need to come into play so that we can really complete the attack that we would like to work with. All of these are different methods that hackers, those who are brand new and those who have been in the game for some time, are able to do. When you are looking to protect your own network or the network for someone else, or you would like to hack onto another network, you will be happy that you have all of these tools ready to help you get this work done.

There are a lot of cool things that we are able to do when it is time to work with the process of hacking, and having this all prepared and ready to go can be one of the best methods you can choose to protect your own network. When you are ready to learn more about hacking and all of the tools and techniques that we are able to use when hacking along with the Kali Linux system, make sure to check out this guidebook to get started.

There are plenty of books on this subject on the market, thanks again for choosing this one! Every effort was made to ensure it is full of as much useful information as possible; please enjoy!

Chapter 1: Definition of Hacking and Types of Hackers

The process of hacking involves getting unauthorized access into a computer system, or a group of computer systems. Hackers get access to systems by cracking codes or passwords. The technique hackers use to obtain code or password is cracking and a hacker is someone that undertakes the process of hacking. Hackers can hack an email account, a social media site, a website, an entire LAN network, or a group of systems. Ultimately, it is through password algorithms programs that the hackers obtain access to a password.

For each of their daily needs, people and also businesses make use of laptops or computers. For a seamless flow of business applications and information, several organizations have WAN, wide area network, website or domain, or a computer network. As a result, there is a high-risk exposure of these networks to hackers as well as the outside world of hacking.

Purpose of Hacking

Mostly, the objective of some hackers is to cause certain reputational or financial harm to an entity, group, or person through their malicious or criminal intent. They achieve this by spreading malicious or incorrect rumors that can cause the disruption of the business after they embezzle their funds or steal their confidential data. Companies can find themselves in some socially detrimental situations with this misleading information. Also, as punishable by law, hacking is a form of internet or cybercrime. However, government law agencies and specific accredited institutions engage in another side of hacking on a professional level. With this case, their intention is to prevent individuals from causing any harm or counter the wrong intentions of the hackers. Also, this type of hacking is done to protect and save the citizens and society at large.

Types of Hackers

It is quite essential for us to differentiate between the objectives and roles of hackers by knowing their types to get the detail on the above-broached objectives.

Hacktivist

Leaving contentious information on a website that they hack is the focus of these types of hackers. They do this to spread religious, social, and political messages. Also, other nations can be targeted by these hackers.

Grey hat

These types of hackers have no intention of fraudulent when they access a system without any authorization. They are between the black and white hat hackers. The objective of these hackers is to show the stakeholders of the system parts of its weaknesses and vulnerabilities.

Ethical Hacker

The objective of these types of hackers is to eliminate and identify suspected weaknesses. They assess systems by getting access as officially and recognized stamped hackers and they are known also as white hat. A few things they also do is to retrieve critical information needed for security purposes, crack codes of anti-social or illegal setups, and vulnerability assessment. They are paid, certified, and trained experts.

The ethical hackers are the only individuals who are allowed to do this kind of hacking legally. They know the same kinds of rules to follow as a black hat hacker and will use some of the same ideas along the way. But they have usually gained permission to go through and do some of these options, rather than trying to do it to gain their own personal advantage.

For the ethical hacker, the goal is to keep the system as safe and secure as possible along the way. They want to either protect their own network, or the network of someone else who knows what they are here. This will make it easier for them to get onto the network without doing so in an illegal manner.

These hackers are going to use a lot of the same methods for their attacks, as we see with some of the other types of hackers. This means that they are going to rely on penetration testing, mapping out attacks, and more. But they are going to do it as a way to help them figure out where the vulnerabilities in the system are rather than looking at ways that you can exploit them.

Cracker

These are black hat. They secure entry into websites or computer networks through an unauthorized manner and also with a mala fide intention. There is also an attachment of personal gain in their intention through privacy rights violations to benefit criminal organizations, stealing of funds from online bank accounts, stealing confidential organizational information, and so on. These days, these hackers engage in their activities in a shady manner and they belong to this category.

Types of Hacking

The threats that websites have to deal with are some of the most frequent threats of hacking. Hackers engage in the process of making the contents of a website public or changed with the use of unauthorized access. The individuals or groups that are opposed to social or political organizations most times target their websites. Also, they hack national or governmental information website, and this is entirely common. Here are some of common the hacking methods they use on the websites:

DNS Spoofing

Sometimes, users might forget about the cache data of a domain or website, and this method of hacking uses this cache data. Then, it points the data to another malicious website.

Cookie Theft

Cookies contain login passwords, confidential information, and so on, and with the use of malicious codes, hackers will have access to the website to steal cookies. When a legitimate company uses these, it is going to help them provide you with a better service overall. But it does store a lot of extra information on you and your system, and if the hacker is able to steal these cookies, they will be able to use them in any manner that they would like. This could be dangerous and is a big reason that it is often best to turn off and disable the use of cookies in the first place.

UI Redress

Hackers use this method by creating a fake user interface. Thus, users will be directed to another website altogether when they click with the intention of going to a specific site.

Virus

When hackers get access to a specific website, they release a virus into the files of the website. Their objectives are to corrupt the resources or information on such a website. There are a lot of different types of viruses that we are able to meet up with, and they can be spread through email attachments, websites that have been compromised, and more.

These viruses can take over the computer, shutting down files, stealing information, and even spreading to some of the contacts that you have on your system to get the information that the hackers would like to have. This is why it is so important to go through and be careful about the kinds of websites that you open, and to make sure that you are not going to websites that could harm your computer.

Phishing

They use this method to replicate the original website, and as such, the hackers will easily seize and misuse the unsuspecting user's information like credit card details, account password, and so many more.

Many times these are going to be sent through email. The email is going to appear as it comes from the legitimate source, such as your bank or another site that you spend some time on, asking for you to check out a message or change your username and password.

Because the hacker does a great job of hiding things and making it look official, it does not take that long for people to fall for it. Even the website is going to look legitimate so it is easy to click on the different items and enter the information. If someone does fall for this, the hacker is able to take all of that information and use it to actually get into the account of yours that they would like.

How Do Hackers Get Access into Computer Systems

We can get information by working and communicating with others through the help of some good guys in the computer world that create networks. And then, for a variety of reasons, we have some not-so-good individuals that cause troubles by using their computers to worm their way into those networks. These set of individuals are hackers and part of the things they engage in include:

- Shut down a website by creating heavy traffic to it
- Obtain credit card information
- Get passwords
- Steal secrets

Whether by disrupting business as usual or stealing information for their gain, hackers are always at work. Every now and then, there will always be news about them, and at a point, you may likely be wondering about just exactly what hackers are doing. They are always getting in the system by stealing passwords. For them to crack the security of a network, the first step for them is to find out a password. As a result, to make your password hard to figure out by anyone, it is quite useful to change them regularly. For you to know what hackers do when people discuss them, here are some key terms that you may probably hear about them:

- **Trojan horse**: this technique appears to be a helpful program and users are tricked into clicking and opening it. But the computers of such users can get unexpected attacks which can be behind the scenes or unnoticed. Because these are going to sneak onto the computer through methods that are secret, such as being on a program that seems legitimate, it is hard to detect them. But when the Trojan horse gets into the system, it can open up back doors and other things to help the hacker get the information that they want.
- **Session hijacking**: this technique involves hackers inserting malicious data packets into an actual data transmission over the internet connection.
- **Script kiddie**: this is unsophisticated or young hackers who act like a real hacker while using hackers' tools. These individuals are not going to care that much about learning how to hack. They want to complete an attack, but they don't really care about the basics that go with it or the codes that they need to use. Instead,

they are going to just take on some of the tools and programs that are already out there and will use these to help them out. They just want to complete the hack and get the information out of it, without having to worry about learning any of the techniques along the way.

- **Root kit**: an intruder can disguise and expand his control over your system by using this set of tools.
- **Root access**: for any hacker to get complete control over a system, root access is the highest level of access. Root access is the most desired by serious hackers to a computer system.
- **Email worm**: hackers use a natural-looking email message to send a mini-program or virus-laden script to an unsuspecting victim.
- **Denial-of-service attack**: hackers use this method to flood a website with false traffic, thereby preventing the system of the victim or crippling it from handling its normal traffic. This one is going to turn down the server for a particular company and can make it hard for legitimate users to get onto the system at all. This allows the hacker to have a chance to leave a Trojan or a back door or something else on that network.
  - ○ **Distributed Denial of Service**: This one is going to be a bit different because it is going to utilize more than one computer to do the attack. In the DoS, the hacker is just using one computer, and the firewall can usually see that IP address and will stop allowing the service from that address. With the DDoS, the hacker is using a lot of different computers to do the process which makes it harder for the firewall to stop the attack.

- **Buffer overflow**: hackers use this method by overrunning an application buffer to deliver malicious commands to a system.
- **Back door**: hackers get access to a computer system using this secret pathway. Trojan horses, viruses, and other types of malware are able to come in and utilize this option to help them get onto the system and come back and forth as many times as they would like. If you are trying to protect your own computer or another system, make sure that when you are all done, you fix it all up so there are no potential back doors for a hacker to get through.

Guarding Against Hacking

A persistent threat that is continuously affecting the security of a nation and its citizens is hacking. At the level of the individual, when hackers wipe away the entire hard-earned financial savings of someone, it can result in untold financial losses. Also, it can lead to long-term repercussions and major financial losses through the theft of data at the organizational level. It is essential to block this vicious menace and safeguard it.

There are a lot of things that you are able to do to make sure that you can keep your own network safe against another hacker. Setting this up well, and being careful about how your own network is going to behave is going to be so important to keep the hackers out. Some of the different steps that you are able to take in order to guard against any hackers that would like to get on your network will include:

1. Be careful about the emails that you use. Many of the attacks that we are going to explore in this guidebook are going to be activated with the help of email. This isn't true all of the time. But if you are careful with some of the emails that you open, especially the attachments, then you can avoid a lot of these attacks from a hacker.

2. Pick out some strong passwords that are harder to guess or get through with a brute force attack. Pick out passwords that are long, use a combination of letters, numbers and symbols, and ones that are not going to be related back to you or easy to guess at all. Many hackers are going to start by trying to attack your passwords because this is a weak point in your security. You can ix this with the help of a strong password.

3. Do a penetration test to look for some of the vulnerabilities that are on the system. We will take a look at how to work with penetration testing later on, but this is a great way to figure out which places the hacker may try to use in order to get onto your network. Doing one for yourself will help to keep it protected.

4. Change passwords on a regular basis. When you change the password on a regular basis, it is a lot harder for the hacker to guess what it is or use some of

the other methods of password cracking to get through with the help of the password.

5. Do not share information about the network with anyone else. Any important and sensitive information about your network needs to be kept secret and hidden. The more people who know about your network, the more likely it is that the information will get out, and a hacker will be able to utilize this.

6. Consider encrypting the information that you send to others in your communications. This makes it hard for anyone who does not have the right key to read any of the information that you are sending, even if it does get intercepted.

7. Pick out a strong security protocol to protect your network. Make sure that you are not working with the WEP option because this one is often easier for a hacker to get through. While the WPA and WPA2 are still options that are vulnerable to an attack, they are a lot stronger and can keep you safer along the way.

8. Use anti-malware and anti-virus software. These will make it harder for any of the attacks that the hacker is trying to send your way to get through.

9. Make sure that you are updating your software and operating system as often as it is needed. These updates are going to help cut out some of the vulnerabilities that are found in the operating system you use, and

other software, so doing the update will make it harder for a hacker to get onto your system.

As you can see, there are going to be a lot of options that you are able to work with when it is time to protect your computer compared to some of the hacks that are coming your way. Make sure to work with some of these options, and you will find that it is a lot harder for a hacker to get on your system and use it for their own advantage along the way.

Chapter 2: Cybersecurity

The practice of defending data, networks, electronic systems, mobile devices, servers, and computers from malicious attacks is cybersecurity. Also, they refer to it as electronic information security or information technology security. Common categories can also fit into the terms as well as a variety of contexts, from mobile to business computing.

- The most unpredictable cybersecurity factor is end-user education. When people fail to follow healthy security practices, they can accidentally introduce a virus to an otherwise secure system. Thus, it is quite vital for the security of any organization to educate its employees not to plug in unidentified USB drives and to delete suspicious email attachments.

- For any causes of loss of data or operations, the manner with which an organization responds to a cybersecurity incident is the business continuity and disaster recovery. And for the organization to return to the same operating capacity as before the event, the processes that dictate how the organization restores its information and operation are the disaster recovery policies. While the organization is attempting to operate without specific resources, the organization has a plan that it falls back on, which is the business continuity.

- The decisions and procedures of protecting and handling data assets are operational security. This process encompasses the activities that determine where and how data may be shared or stored and the users' permissions while accessing a network.
- When data is in transit or in storage, the privacy and integrity of data are protected by the information security.
- For devices and software to be free of threats is the focus of the application security. Even though it is designed to protect data, a compromised application could provide access to the data. Before the deployment of a device or program, the design phase is the beginning of the successful security.
- Irrespective of if an attack may come from opportunistic malware or targeted attackers, the practice of securing a computer network from intruders is the network security.

Cyber Threat Scale

Every year, about $19 billion is spent by the U.S. government on cybersecurity. However, the pace at which the cyber-attacks are evolving is quite fast. According to NIST, the National Institute of Standards and Technology, real-time monitoring of all electronic resources is recommended to aid in early detection and combat the proliferation of malicious code. Cybersecurity counter three-fold threats and they are:

1. To cause fear or panic, the intention of cyberterror is to undermine electronic systems
2. Most times, politically motivated information gathering is involved in cyber-attacks
3. For financial gain or to cause disruption, groups or single actors can target systems through cybercrime.

Ransomware, Trojans, spyware, worms, and viruses are some of the common techniques attackers utilize to control networks or computers. For surreptitious data collection, they make use of Trojans and spyware and to damage or self-replicate systems or files. They use worms or viruses. All the information of the user is encrypted by ransomware, who waits for an opportunity to do so, and for the use to get access to their encrypted information, there will be demands for payment. A legitimate-looking download can contain a malware payload and they use it and also unsolicited email attachment to spread malicious code.

Irrespective of size, all industries have their fair share of the cybersecurity. In recent years, government, finance, manufacturing, and healthcare are some of the industries that reported the most cyberattacks. Since these industries collect medical and financial data, several of these sectors are more appealing to cybercriminals. However, they can also target all businesses that use networks for customer attacks, corporate espionage, and customer data.

More than before, the world relies on technology. As such, there is a surge in digital data creation. Today, computers are used to store a great deal of that data by governments and businesses, and they transmit it across networks to other computers. There is vulnerability in devices and their underlying systems that undermine the objectives and health of an organization when exploited. For any business, there can be a range of devastating consequences with a data breach. Through the loss of partner and consumer trust, a data breach can unravel the reputation of a company. A company can lose its competitive advantage through the loss of vital data such as intellectual property or source files. Also, because of non-compliance with data protection regulations, corporate revenue can be impacted through a data breach. About $3.6 million is the average cost that a data breach can cost an affected organization. It is quite critical for organizations to implement and adopt a strong cybersecurity approach with high-profile data breaches making media headlines.

Advancement of Cybersecurity

The focus of traditional cybersecurity is on the implementation of defensive measures around a defined perimeter. BYOD, Bring Your Own Device and remote workers are the recent enablement initiatives that have expended the attack surface, reduced the visibility into cyber activity, and dissolved the perimeter. Today, despite the record levels of security spending, there is a rapid increment in breaches. The focus is on human-centric cybersecurity for a global organization. It is a new approach that, instead of an exponential number of growing threats, places focus on changes in user behavior. Where data resides, human-centric cybersecurity extends security controls into all the systems and also offers insight into the manner with which an end-user interacts with data even when the organization is not in control exclusively. Ultimately, to reduce threat detection and investigation times as well as prioritize and surface the most serious threats, this approach is designed to identify behavioral anomalies.

Protecting the End-User

So, what are the security measures provided by cybersecurity for systems and users? First, to encrypt files, emails, and other vital data, cybersecurity relies on cryptographic protocols. Not only does this technique guard against theft or loss, but it also protects information in transit. Also, the computer is scanned by the end-user security software for pieces of malicious code, quarantines this code, and then deletes it from the system. For malicious code hidden in MBR, Master Boot Record with a specific design to wipe or encrypt data from the hard drive of computers, security programs can also remove them after it has detected them. There is also a focus on real-time malware detection by electronic security protocols. For some to monitor the behavior of a program and its code to defend against Trojans and viruses that change their shape with each execution, both metamorphic and polymorphic malware, they make use of behavioral analysis and heuristic. From the network of a user, security programs can confine potentially malicious programs to a virtual bubble to learn how to better detect new infections and analyze their behavior. And as experts of cybersecurity identify new ways to combat new threats, security programs continue to evolve new defenses.

Chapter 3: Types of Cyber Attacks

With the use of several techniques to destroy, alter, or steal information or data systems, any targeted offensive action that focuses on personal, computer devices, infrastructures, or computer information systems is a cyberattack. Without further ado, here are some of the common cyberattacks today:

Birthday Attack

The creation of the birthday attacks is developed against hash algorithms which people use to confirm the integrity of a digital signature, software, or a message. A fixed length MD, message digest, which is independent of the input message length, is produced by a processed hash function message. The message has the characteristics of this MD uniquely. The probability of finding two random messages is the reference for the birthday attack, which, when processed by a hash function, generates the same MD. The attacker can safely replace the message of the user with his if the attacker calculates a similar MD for the message as the user has. And even if they compare MDs, the receiver will not be able to detect the replacement.

Eavesdropping Attack

Attackers intercept the network traffic for the eavesdropping attack to happen. For some confidential information that a user might be sending over the network such as credit card numbers and passwords, an attacker can obtain those data by eavesdropping. There are two types of eavesdropping attackers, and they are active and passive:

- Active eavesdropping: by sending queries to transmitters, the attackers will disguise themselves as friendly units as they actively grab the information. They call this process as tampering, scanning, or probing.
- Passive eavesdropping: when attackers listen to the message transmission in the network, they will detect the information.

Also, since by conducting passive eavesdropping before active attacks require the attacker to gain knowledge of the friendly units, quite essential than spotting active ones is detecting passive eavesdropping attacks. To guard against eavesdropping, the best countermeasure is data encryption.

XSS, Cross-Site Scripting Attack

For running scriptable applications or scripts in the web browser of the victim, it is the third-party web resources that the XSS attacks use. Essentially, the attacker will use malicious JavaScript by injecting a payload into the database of a website. Using the payload of the attacker as part of the HTML body, the website will transmit the page to the browser of the victim to execute the malicious script when the victim requests a page from the website. For example, the attacker can use the cookie from the server of the attacker after extracting it for session hijacking when it sends this cookie of the victim. When they use XSS to exploit more vulnerability, there can be the most dangerous consequences. Attackers can control and access the machine of the victim remotely, collect as they discover network information, capture screenshots, or log keystrokes in addition to stealing cookies through these vulnerabilities. Since there is a wide support for JavaScript on the web, it is the most widely abused while, within Flash, ActiveX, and VBScript, they can take advantage of XSS.

Data input can be sanitized by the developers when users in an HTTP request before reflecting it back to defend against XSS attacks. And before echoing back anything to the user, it is essential to see that all data is escaped, filtered, and validated, including the values of query parameters during searchers. Special characters like >, <, /, &, ?, spaces can be converted to their respective URL encoded equivalent of HTML. Users can have the option of disabling client-side scripts.

SQL Injection Attack

For websites that are database-driven, one common issue is the SQL injection. The process happens when, from client to server, a malefactor executes a SQL query to the database through the input data. In order to run predefined SQL commands, it is possible to insert SQL commands into data-plane input, for example, instead of the password or login. From the database, sensitive data can be exploited by a successful SQL injection. Also, it can issue commands to the operating system, recover the content of a given file, execute administration operations like shutdown on the database, and also modify (delete, update, or insert) database data. For example, the account of a user can be requested by a web form on a website and then to pull up the connected account information using dynamic SQL, send it to the database. The process can leave a hole for attackers even when this works for users who are properly entering their account number.

There is no specific distinction between the data and control planes with the vulnerability to this type of cybersecurity attack. Thus, if a site utilizes dynamic SQL, SQL injections can work mostly. Also, because of the prevalence of older functional interfaces, SQL injection is quite common with ASP and PHP applications. And due to the availability of the programmatic interface nature, the less likely easily exploited SQL injections are ASP.NET and J2EE. In your database, apply the leastoprivilege model of permission to protect yourself from a SQL injection attacks. It is vital not to include any dynamic SQL as you adhere to the process and parameterized queries for the prepared statements. And to prevent injection attacks, you will require a strong database for the executed code. Also, at the application level, it is vital to validate input data against a white list.

Password Attack

Obtaining passwords tend to be the effective and common attack approaches since to authenticate users to an information system, passwords are the most commonly used mechanism. Through outright guessing, gaining access to a password database, using social engineering, acquiring unencrypted passwords by sniffing the connection to the network, or looking around the desk of a person, attackers can get access to the password of a person. Then, they can use a systematic or random manner to execute the last approach.

- Using the **dictionary attack**, attack attempts to gain access to the network or computer of a user by using a dictionary of common passwords. Attackers may compare the results after applying similar encryption to a commonly used password dictionary as they copy an encrypted file that contains the passwords.
- Attackers may hope that one password will work after using a random approach to guess different passwords. This process is called **Brute-force**. The process tends to be logical for attackers when they use hobbies, title, job, name, and similar terms of the person to guess passwords related to the person.

An account lockout policy that will lock your account after some invalid password attempts is all that is needed to protect yourself from brute-force and dictionary attacks.

Drive-By Attack

The prevalent technique to spread malware is the drive-by download attacks. On one of the pages, attackers will have a malicious script planted into PHP or HTTP code. With this planted, the script could redirect the victim to a site controlled by the hackers or might install malware directly onto the visitor's computer. When viewing or visiting a pop-up window or an email message or when you are visiting a website, drive-by downloads can take place. You can be infected with a drive-by attack even if you don't open a malicious email attachment or click on a download button. For you to enable the attack, you may not necessarily have to do anything, which makes drive-by attack different from other kinds of cybersecurity attacks. Due to a lack of updates or unsuccessful updates, a drive-by download can take advantage of a web browser, operating system, or an app that contained security flaws.

You may be required to avoid websites that could contain malicious code and keep your operating systems or browsers up to date to guard yourself against drive-by attacks. Even though those websites are liable to hacking, try to stick to the sites you use normally. And always delete unnecessary apps or programs from your device. Drive-by attacks can exploit more vulnerability on your system when you have more plug-ins.

Phishing and Spear Phishing Attacks

The purpose of a phishing attack is to influence users to do something or gain personal information by sending an email that seems to originate from trusted sources. This type of attack utilizes technical trickery and social engineering. Malware can be loaded into your computer through an attachment of an email. Also, you can be tricked into handing over your personal information or downloading the malware through a link to an illegitimate website. A phishing activity that is quite targeted is spear phishing. A bit of research goes into the targets by the attacker, after which relevant and personal messages are created. Spear phishing appears to be quite hard to be identified and guarding against it can also be harder. Email spoofing is one of the simplest approaches hackers use to conduct a spear-phishing attack. They make the email seem like it is coming from a known person like your partner or management since they have falsified the information in the section "From" of the email. Also, website cloning is another method that scammers use to infuse credibility to their story. They will fool you to enter login credentials or personally identifiable information, PII.

Here are some methods you can engage in cutting down on the risk of phishing:

- **Sandboxing**: you can make use of a sandbox environment to test the content of the email, clicking the links inside the email, or logging activity from opening the attachment
- **Email header analysis**: how an email got to your address is the purpose of email headers. As is stated in the email, there must be similarity in the domain of the "Return-Path" and the "Reply-to" parameters.
- **Hovering over the links**: don't attempt to click it when you move your mouse over the link. You will know where it will actually take you when you hover your mouse over the link, and to decipher the URL, you will need to apply critical thinking.
- **Critical thinking**: just because you have 200 other unread messages in your inbox or you are stressed or busy, you will take it that an email is the real deal. You will want to take a minute to analyze the email.
-

MitM, Man-in-the-Middle Attack

In the situation where a hacker plants itself between a server and the communications, a MitM attack is happening. Some of the man-in-the-middle attack types include:

Replay

Attackers can impersonate one of the participants by intercepting and saving old messages and attempt to send them later; thereby, a replay attack is taking place. You can use a string that changes later or a random number to counter which nonce or session timestamps to easily counter it.

IP Spoofing

IP spoofing happens when a system provides the attacker with access to it, thinking that it is communicating with a trusted, known entity. A target host gets a trusted, known host from the attacker who, instead of its own IP source address, sends a packet with such an IP source. It is possible for the target host to act upon it after accepting the packet.

Session Hijacking

Between the network server and a trusted client, attackers can hijack a session in this type of MitM attack. While the belief of the server is that of a communication with the client as it continues the session, there will be a substitution of the IP address of the attacking computer for the trusted client. For example, the process of the attack can go thus:

1. There is a connection by the client to a server.
2. The client's control is gained by the computer of the attacker.
3. The computer of the attacker disconnects the client from the server.
4. The attacker uses their IP address to replace that of the IP address of the client, thereby, spoofing the sequence numbers of the client.
5. There is a continuous dialog by the computer of the attacker with the server, and the belief of the server is that the communication still continues with the client.

For the prevention of all MitM attacks at present, there is no configuration or single technology to do the magic. Overall, effective safeguards against MitM attacks are digital certification and encryption, with both assuring integrity and confidentiality of communications. However, that encryption might not help with the way attackers will inject a man-in-the-middle attack. For example, the public key of a man named Greg may be intercepted by an attacker and as such, makes the substitution of that key as his key. Then, anyone could unknowingly use the substituted public key by the attacker, thinking they are sending an encrypted message to Greg. Therefore, the intended message for Greg can be read by the attacker and then uses the genuine Greg's encrypted key to send the message to Greg, and Greg will never notice that the message has been compromised. Also, before sending the message to Greg, the attacker can modify the message. Ultimately, because of the MitM attack, Greg will believe that his information is protected since he is using encryption.

Now, how do you distinguish between the ownership of the public key between the two of them? Solving such a problem like this instigates the development of hash functions and certificate authorities. The following technique can be utilized when someone wants to be sure that an attacker will not see a message they want to send to Greg and that the message will indeed come from that message without any modification from an attacker:

1. A symmetric key will be encrypted by the person after they have created it with their own public key.

2. Then, the person will forward the encrypted symmetric key to Greg.
3. After that, the person will digitally sign a hash function of the message that they have computed.
4. Then, with the use of the symmetric key, the person will encrypt the signed hash message and their message and then sends forward the whole thing to Greg.
5. Since only Greg has the private key to decrypt the encryption, Greg will be able to receive the symmetric key from the person.
6. Since he has the symmetric key, the only person that can decrypt the symmetric signed hash and encrypted message is Greg.
7. And because Greg can compare the received message's hash with digitally signed one and can compute the hash of the received message, Greg can confirm that the message has not been altered.
8. Since only the person can sign the hash for it to verify with the person's public key, Greg can also prove to himself that the person was the sender.

DoS, Denial-of Service, and DDoS Distributed Denial-of-Service Attacks

When the resources of a system cannot respond to service requests, it means a denial-of-service attack has overwhelmed such a system. Though, the attacker controls the malicious software that they have infected in a large number of other host machines, the attack of a DDoS is also on the resources of a system. Attackers don't gain direct benefit from denial-of-service, unlike attacks that they developed to increase or gain access. DoS attacks satisfy some of the attackers. However, there may be real enough benefits for attackers if the attacked resources belong to a business competitor. Also, for attackers to launch a new type of attack, they tend to result in DoS attacks to take a system offline. Here are some of the various kinds of DDoS and DoS attacks:

Botnets

For hackers to implement DDoS attacks, they can inflect millions of systems with malware using botnets. And to carry out the attacks against the target systems, they use these bots or zombie systems. Most times, these will overwhelm the processing capacity and bandwidth of the target system. And since the locations of the botnets are quite differing, it can be difficult to trace these DDoS attacks. The mitigation of botnets can arise through:

- Using black hole filtering. Before it enters a protected network, it drops undesirable traffic. The host of the Border Gateway Protocol is required to forward routing updates to ISP routers in the event of detecting a DDoS attack. At the next hop, nullo interface will receive all traffic heading to victim servers.
- To deny traffic from spoofed addresses, using RFC3704 filtering, which its correct source network can be traced for that traffic. For example, from bogon

list addresses, packets will be dropped by RFC3704 filtering.

Ping of Death Attack

Ping of death attacks makes use of an IP size over the maximum of 65,535 bytes to ping a target system using IP packets. The IP packet is fragmented by the attackers since IP packets of this size are not allowed. Then, other crashes can ensue as well as buffer overflow when the target system reassembles the packet. When you use a firewall, you can block the attack of the ping of death as the IP packets that have been fragmented will be checked for maximum size.

Smurf Attack

Attackers saturate a target network with traffic with the ICMP as well as using IP spoofing with this attack. Attackers target the broadcast IP addresses with the use of ICMP echo requests. As such, the origin of these ICMP requests is from the address of a spoofed victim. For example, for the attackers to broadcast address 10.255.255.255, the attacker would spoof an ICMP echo request from 10.0.0.10 if the intended victim address is 10.0.0.10. All IPs in the range will get this request, and it would overwhelm the network since all the responses are going back to 10.0.0.10. Not only can this method generate a vast amount of network congestion, but it can also be automated as it can be repeatable. You may want to disable IP-directed broadcasts at the routers for you to protect your devices from this attack. Then, you will be able to protect the ICMP echo broadcast request at the network devices. Also, to keep them from responding to ICMP packets from broadcast addresses, another option is to configure the end systems.

Teardrop Attack

Attackers use this method to offset fields in sequential Internet Protocol packets by causing the fragmentation and length to overlap one another on the attacked host. Though it will fail, during the process, there will be an attempt by the attacked system to reconstruct packets. Then, the system will crash eventually due to confusion. You may want to block ports 445 and 139 as you disable SMBv2 for you to protect against this DoS attack if you don't have patches.

TCP SYN Flood Attack

It is during a TCP session initialization handshake when attackers exploit the use of the buffer space that they use this attack. The small in-process queue if the target system will be flooded with connection requests from the device of the attackers. However, when the target system replies to those requests, it doesn't respond. And while waiting for the response from the device of the attacker, the process will cause the target system to time out. Ultimately, when the connection queue fills up, it makes the system to become unusable or crash. For you to countermeasure a TCPSYN flood attacks, here are some preventions:

- On open connections, decrease the timeout, and increase the size of the connection queue
- For you to stop inbound SYN packets, place servers behind a firewall configured

Chapter 4: Types of Malware

The unwanted software that someone installs in your system without your consent is the precise definition of malicious software. There can be a legitimate attachment of this software to propagate and code, meaning that, across the Internet, it can replicate itself or lurk useful applications. A few common malware types include:

Spyware

They use spyware to collect user's browsing habits, their computer, as well as their information. And without your knowledge, spyware tracks everything you do, and a remote user gets those data. Also, spyware can have malicious programs from the Internet installed or downloaded. When you install another freeware application, spyware is usually a separate program that is installed unknowingly and its working is quite similar to adware.

Adware

Companies use adware, a software application for marketing purposes. When any program is running, there will be a display of the advertising banners. While you browse any website, you can download adware automatically to your computer. On the screen of your computer, through a bar or pop-up, you can view it.

Ransomware

This type of malware threatens to delete or publish the data of the victim after blocking them unless there will be payment of a ransom by the victim. The more advanced malware utilizes the cryptoviral extortion technique. Doing this will encrypt the files of the victim and without the decryption key, makes it almost impossible to recover. It can be quite hard for a knowledgeable individual to reverse the lock on the system with the use of some simple computer ransomware.

Droppers

For the installation of viruses on computers, they make use of a program called a dropper. Virus-scanning software cannot detect a dropper since it is not affected by malicious code in several instances. Also, for virus software that is resident on a compromised system, a dropper can connect to the internet and download updates.

Worms

Worms propagate across computers and networks as self-contained programs, and since they have no attachment to a host file, they differ from viruses. They use email attachment to spread worms and it gets activated when you open the program. Apart from conducting malicious activities, the worm can also send a copy of itself to all contact of the email address of an infected computer. Then, there can be an event of denial-of-service attacks against nodes on the network when a worm spreads across the internet and overload email servers.

Logic Bombs

Appended to an application is a type of malicious software, which is a logic bomb. A specific occurrence triggers it such as a specific time and date or a logical condition.

Trojans

Usually, Trojans has a malicious function and are hidden in a useful program. Since Trojans do not replicate, this major trait separates it from viruses. Also, attackers can exploit a backdoor established by a Trojan to launch attacks on a system. For example, so hackers can perform an attack after using it to listen, they can program a Trojan to open a high-numbered port.

Stealth Viruses

For stealth viruses to conceal themselves, they take over the functions of a system. The report of the software is that of uninfected since they have compromised the malware detection. They change the time and date of the last modification of the file and conceal any increase in the size of an infected file.

Polymorphic Viruses

When the viruses vary cycles of decryption and encryption, they use this process to conceal themselves. So, initially decrypted by a decryption program is a connected mutation engine and the encrypted virus. A code area will be thus be infected by the encrypted virus. Then, there will be a development of a new decryption routine by the mutation engine. Using an algorithm corresponding to the new decryption routine, a copy of the virus and the mutation engine will then be encrypted by the virus. The new code will then have an attachment of the encrypted package of virus and mutation engine. Thus, the process continues to repeat itself. It is quite tricky to detect such viruses. However, due to the several modifications of their source code, they have a high level of entropy. For quick detection, you can use Process Hacker.

System or Boot-Record Infections

The hard disks will give a record of a boot-record by the virus attached to the master boot. So it can propagate to other computers and disks, it will look at the boot sector and load the virus into memory when you start the system.

File Infectors

These types of viruses associate themselves with executable code like .exe files. As the code loads, the virus will be installed. And with the creation of a virus file with a similar name, which is an .exe extension, another version of a file infector will connect itself with a file. Thus, the virus code will execute when the file is opened.

Macro Viruses

Those that get infected by these viruses are applications like Excel or Microsoft Word. Macro viruses attach to the initialization sequence of an application. Before it transfers control to the application, the virus executes instructions when the application is opened. In the computer system, there will be a replication of the virus before it attaches to other codes.

Chapter 5: How the Hacking Process Works

System information leakage is the primary use of hacking before. There is now dark connotation connected to hack in the recent years, courtesy of some villain players. On the other hand, for them to be assured of their systems' weaknesses and strengths, hackers are employed by various corporations to do this. They earn a fat salary through a positive trust they build, and also, they are aware of the point that they need to stop. So, without further ado, let's make a deep dive into the art of hacking.

Preparation Phase

A programming language is highly required here. Though you will see some essential guidelines, you must not restrict yourself to a specific language. Tolerance is quite needed in this stage because it might take time to learn programming language.

- It is compulsory to know assembly language. Though there are several variables of it, your processor understands only this language. Also, when you don't know assembly, exploiting a program may not be possible.
- You will also need to know bash scripting. The manipulation of Linux/Unix systems will be done with ease, including getting most of the job done for you through writing scripts.
- Since PHP is what most web applications use, you must try to learn PHP, and also, in this field, a reasonable choice for you is perl.
- You can also automate several tasks with powerful, high-level scripting languages like Ruby and Python.
- The languages they used in building Windows and Linux are C++ and C. most especially; it teaches how memory works and also assemble language.

Then, your target needs to be in the picture. This process is referred to as enumeration, which is how you will gather vital information about your target. You will have fewer surprises when you know more about your target in advance.

Now, the process of hacking can begin. For your commands, put a *nix terminal into use. For users of Windows, a *nix will help in emulation through Cygwin. Nmap doesn't need Cygwin as it runs on Windows and uses WinPCap. However, because of the lack of raw sockets, Nmap doesn't work well on Windows systems. Also, because of their flexibility, BSD and Linux must be in your list of considerations. And there are several pre-installed tools with several Linux distributions. Alternatively, in the Windows Store, you can find a *nix terminal on Windows 10 fall Creators Updates or later and courtesy of Windows Linux Subsystem, the Linux command-line can be emulated by Windows.

Now, the first step is to secure your system. For you to give enough protection to yourself, you need to quite understand all common techniques. You need an authorization from your target for you to attack as you begin with the fundamentals. You can do this by using virtual machines to set up your laboratory, ask for written permission from your target, or even attack your network. You will get in trouble if you attempt to attack a network because it is illegal, no matter its content.

The process of testing your target is the next stage. Will you be able to get to the remote system? Though it is what most operating systems use, the result of using the ping utility to be sure your target is alive may not be quite concrete. Paranoid administrators of systems can easily shut it off since it relies on the ICMP protocol. Then, you will need to define the OS. When you intend to run a port scan, try nmap or pOf. So you can make your plan of action; running a scan of the ports will tell you the kind of router or firewall your target is using and you will see the ports that are open on the OS and the machine. Then, you can use the -o switch to activate OS detection in nmap.

By now, you would have discovered an open port or a path in the system. Most times, there is a strong protection for certain ports like HTTP (80) and FTP (20).

- The evidence of a secure shell, SSH, service running on the target is an open port 22, and this can be brute force sometimes.
- It is possible your target could have forgotten other UDP and TCP ports, including several UDP ports left open for LAN gaming and also Telnet.

The next process is the authentication after you must have cracked the password. Brute force is among several techniques you can use to crack a password. You can try every potential password that a predefined dictionary of brute force software contains.

- Most times, finding your way into a system tends to be much easier even without cracking the password
- For you to upload it to the secure site, you can go for a TCP scan installation or acquire a rooted tablet. Then, you will cause the password to appear on your proxy when the IP address opens
- It may not be a good idea to attempt a login to a remote machine using every possible password. While it may take some time to complete, it could pollute the system logs, and intrusion detection systems can detect it easily

- For you to crack password quickly, you may result in using Rainbow Tables. You need to understand that it is only if the hash of the password is in your possession can the password cracking be a good method
- As it is thousands of times faster, another processor is the newer techniques that use the graphics card
- You can get a massive speed boost by cutting the MD5 algorithms and also exploiting the weaknesses of most hashing algorithms can significantly improve the speed of the cracking since they are generally weak
- Brute force can take a lot of time since users are using strong passwords. However, brute force techniques have improved with several major improvements

The privilege of a super-user is what you need to get now. If it is a Windows system you are trying to crack, you will need administrator privileges, and if your target is a *nix machine, the root privileges are all you need.

- You may not be able to access all the features of a connection that you gain access into. However, you can do everything if you have the root, administrator, or super-user account
- Except it has been altered, the admin account comes by default for routers, and it is administrator account for Windows
- You may require a specific level of authentication for you to get the most information because they have all been protected. You will require super-user privileges to see all the files on a computer. In BSD and Linux OS, root users get similar privileges as a user account

Now, you may want to engage in some different tricks. Most times, you may want to bump up your authorization level by causing the memory to dump so you can inject code or perform a task at a higher level by creating a buffer overflow to gain super-user status.

- You can do this by finding or writing an insecure program that you can execute on their machine
- If the bugged software has setuid bit set, this will happen in Unix-like systems, and as such, it is as a super-user that the program will be executed

You may want to have a backdoor developed at this stage. It tends to be ideal that you can come back again when you have gained complete access to a system. You can backdoor certain essential system services like the SSH server. Though, during the next upgrade of the system, your backdoor may be removed. Then, the solution is to backdoor also the compiler itself so you have a possible way of coming back through every compiled software. And your tracks must be covered. It is quite critical that the system administrator knows nothing about the compromise of the system. Never have more than necessary files created or make a change to the website. Also, you don't need to create more users. Make fast actions. Ensure that your secret password is hard-coded anytime you patch a server like SSHD. Though without containing any crucial information, the server must let them in if anyone attempts to login with this password.

Chapter 6: Why Hackers Use Linux

There are several special features on the Linux operating system that make it more dominating than any other OS. With Unix as its old version, the operating system of Linux is an open source. Day by day, there is a rapid development in the use of Linux. And rather than using any other operating systems such as Mac or Windows, hackers like to use Linux because of the additional benefits Linux operating system has over others. The operating system of Linux has remarkable special features that make it more dominating than other systems even though their operating systems are more user-friendly.

Why Hackers Prefer Linux Operating System

For the challenge of it, and because they want to make money from their natural hacking capacities, hackers break into the networks of computers or standalone personal computer systems. And to test their skills, hackers will need the operating system, which offers maximum security. Thus, Linux appears to be the best choice for hackers since it makes it more secure for them in all of their activities. For libraries and Linux applications, they have written millions of lines of code today. This process has allowed it to be integrated into broadly diverse projects as it is done in an extremely modular manner. For example, you can have a part of a library used as a network hijacking code, even with it allowing you to sniff the network for proactive performance monitoring. Also, network security can be hacked with ease.

As it is flexible, hackers have the opportunity of playing their entire fashionable activities using the playground of Linux. Also, it is quite simple for hackers to understand, learn, and use Linux since they can use their penetrating testing methods to know if there is insecurity. Linux is quite secure since when problems arise, hackers can patch it because they have the ability to look at each and every line of Linux code. It can also be used at any time by any user working on it and not only some programmers working in some corporate organizations. Here are some of the benefits of Linux over others:

Easy to Use

The general belief is that Linux is only for hackers and programmers, and that tends to be the widespread myth. However, this analog is far from being the truth. You will easily have a basic understanding of Linux if you have been using it for some time. It is not the same as the operating system of Windows. As such, it could be quite tricky when we make the switch to a different operating system. You will find Linux to be user-friendly and more convenient than Windows.

Less RAM Consumption

Linux consumes lesser processing utility and RAM as well as requires lesser space for disk since it is quite light. Thus, you can have other operating systems such as Windows and OS X installed with it.

Linux is the Future

First, Android is based on Linux and also, the choice for web servers is the Linux operating system for its robustness, flexibility, and stability.

No Requirement for Drivers

You don't need separate drivers before you can use Linux. Within the Linux kernel, you will find all the necessary drivers you will need when you install Linux. As a result, to install drivers for hardware, you won't need CDs anymore.

Serious Take on Privacy

All over the Internet, many people are talking about Windows 10 and the issue of privacy. Usually, your data is collected by

Windows 10. However, there is no case of anyone collecting information and data about you for monetary gain when you use Linux operating system.

Hacking Tools are Often Written for Linux

Nmap and Metasploit, some of the popular hacking tools are ported for Windows. However, Linux has some better tools and in a much better way, manages memory, and not all capabilities are transferred from Linux.

Several Programming Languages Have the Support of Linux

Most programming languages have abundant support from Linux. On Linux, working perfectly are Perl, Python, Ruby, PHP, Java, and C++/C. It is effective and simple when you want to use Linux for any of the scripting languages.

Less Vulnerable

There is so much vulnerability in virtually all the operating systems available except Linux. Linux has fewer vulnerabilities, and it prides itself as the most secure operating system.

Low Cost

It is widely known that Linux is an open-source operating system and so, you can get it online for free as well as freely install and use app the applications without any payment.

Flexibility

You can use Linux for high-performance desktop and server applications, as well as embedded systems.

Maintenance

It is quite easy to maintain the operating system of Linux. You can install all the software with ease. It is even easier to search for their software since every variant of Linux has its central software repository.

Portable and Light

From nearly any Linux distribution that they want, the customized live boot drives and disks are there for hackers to develop. Since the resources it consumes are quite fewer, it is quick to install. The fact that it consumes fewer resources makes Linux light-weight.

Command-Line Interface

Windows and Mac don't have the specially designed, highly-integrated, and strong command-line interface which Linux boasts of having. Other Linux users and hackers will have control over their system with greater access.

Multitasking

All at the same time, you can make use of Linux, as that is how it is designed. For example, your other works will not experience any form of slowdown with a large printing job in the background. Also, your primary processes will not be disturbed even with several works done at the same time.

Network Friendly

Linux is effective in managing network over it since it offers several commands and libraries that hackers use to test network penetrations. Hence, as an open-source operating system, the team that contributes to it does so over the internet network. Also, more than any other operating system, Linux makes network backup faster as a reliable operating system.

Stability

When you want to maintain performance levels, the only OS that doesn't require any periodic rebooting is Linux. Also, the cause of memory leaks cannot slow it down or make it freeze up too. For many years, you can continue to use this operating system.

Since hackers can increase their hacking capabilities and also test their skills on this operating system, it makes Linux as their best choice. The setup programs and installation is user-friendly, and several Linux distributions have tools that make installation of more software quite user-friendly.

Chapter 7: Kali Linux Installation and Updates

A security-focused operating system is one of the most essential things to have when you are looking for a career in information security. You can efficiently perform tedious and time-consuming tasks with the help of a suitable operating system. At present, the operating systems of Linux are indeed countless. However, one of the best choices is Kali Linux. cybersecurity professionals use it for assessing network security, ethical hacking, and penetration testing.

Kali Linux will be one of the first names to be mentioned when it comes to offensive Linux distributions, hacking, and penetration testing. There are several information security tasks as various command-line hacking tools that Linux comes pre-packaged like application security, computer forensics, network security, and penetration testing.

Fundamentally, when you attempt to engage in ethical hacking, the operating system of Linux is an ultimate solution.

Kali Linux Installation

The process of installing Kali Linux can be quite simple, and the options of installation are numerous. The techniques most people prefer are:

1. Using the operating system to dual boot Kali Linux
2. With virtualization software like VirtualBox or VMware
3. Installation of hard disk for Kali Linux
4. Making a Kali Linux bootable USB drive while installing Kali Linux

The focus will be on using virtualization software to install Kali Linux even while there are several options available. For you to perform a comprehensive penetration test using all the tools you need, you can set up your machine by following these steps.

Requirements for Installation

- USB support / DVD-CD drive
- While working with VirtualBox or VMware, the recommendation is around 4 GB
- The recommendation for your hard drive is a minimum free space of 20 GB

The Installation Process

Step 1: VMware installation:

First, a kind of virtualization software is essential to run Kali Linux. For many people, there is a preference for VMware even when they can use VirtualBox by Oracle as part of several options that they can choose from. From your applications folder, launch VMware when you have finished with the installation.

Step 2: Kali Linux download and image integrity checking:

You can choose the one that best suits your needs when you go to the official download page to download Kali Linux. Also, there are some hexadecimal numbers on the download page. There is nothing so important about them. Also, for the tasks that are related to security is the intention of Kali Linux. As such, the integrity checking of your downloaded image is highly required. The file's SHA-256 fingerprint needs to be checked and make a comparison with the one you see on the site you make the download.

Step 3: a new virtual machine launch:

You will hit the 'create a new virtual machine' button when you get to the homepage of the VMware Workstation Pro. Before you configure the details of virtual machine, you must have chosen the guest operating system after selecting the iso file of Kali Linux. Choose the Kali Linux VM to start the virtual machine, and you will click on the green button with 'power on' inscription. You will see the machine starting up!

The process of installation

In the GRUB menu, you will get the prompt to choose your preferred mode of installation when the machine is powered up. Before you continue, choose the graphical installation. You will be taken to another page where you will be prompted to choose your layout for the keyboard, the location of your country, and the language you prefer. Then, the loader will have the related settings of your network configured after installing extra components when you are through with the local information. Then, for this installation, a domain and hostname will be prompted by the installer. Before you continue with the installation, you will have to provide the appropriate information for the environment. You will press continue when you have set a password for the Kali Linux machine. An important note here: make sure you keep your password carefully! Then, set your time zone will be prompted by the installer after you must have set your password. At the partitioning of the disk, it will pause. From the disk partition, four choices will be provided to you by the installer. The 'guided – use entire disk' option is the easiest of them all. For additional granular configuration options, the method of 'manual' partitioning can only be used by experienced users. If you are a new user, the recommendation is to choose all files when you are choosing the partitioning disk and you can click on 'continue.' Then, on the host machine, the entire changes you want to make can then be confirmed. You must be careful here since you can have the data on the disk erased if you continue.

So, the process of file installation will be run through by the installer when you confirm the changes in the partition. As this process can take some minutes, the installation will be done automatically. If you prefer to obtain future pieces of updates and software, the setup for a network mirror will be inquired by the system when the necessary files are installed. If you want to use the repositories of Kali, make sure you have this functionality enabled. Then, the related files of the package manager will be configured. Next, the boot loader of GRUB is the next thing you will be asked to install. Choose 'yes,' and since it will be required to boot Kali, you will choose the device to write the important information for boot loader to the hard drive. To finish the installation, hit the 'continue' button when the installation of GRUB to the disk has finished. Then, specific files for the final stage will be installed. By now, brace up yourself because your journey of exploring Kali Linux has just begun since you have successfully installed Kali.

Updating Kali Linux

The packages index list is the first step of an update for your Kali Linux system. You will enter the following command when you open the terminal;

```
$ sudo apt update
```

As an option, for all scheduled packages for update, you can display them. You have the opportunity of upgrading all packages at once with the use of `apt install PACKAGE-NAME` as well as individual package upgrade at this stage. Now, you have completely upgraded your Kali Linux.

Chapter 8: Installing Kali Linux on Virtual Machine

In similar hardware that you currently have, you can run different operating systems in a number of ways. And some of the options available for you are hard disks, USBs, and DVDs. In this chapter, the assumption is that for you to run your Kali Linux, you have no dedicated computer and as such, we are going to use a virtual PC or a virtualized environment to run it. You must have had virtual box installed on your computer for us to begin the process. And in case you don't have it on your system, it is free to download when you go to the official website of VirtualBox. For the hardware that we will be using to install Kali Linux, this software will be emulating this hardware.

It is widely known that unless you have access to software, it can be quite tricky to download such software. Thus, you will download Kali Linux ISO image from its official page. And in case you want to follow along as you mirror that, the flavor of the Kali Linux KDE 64-bit is what we will be using. The size of its download is around 3.2 GB, and for you to download, it might take a while. You will then have the .ISO image mounted into the virtual machine when you have dealt with that one. If you have the intention of using it in another machine, you can have it burned into a USB or bootable DVD. However, you may need to take into account certain considerations. Then, you may open VirtualBox when the image is downloaded.

Now, you will hit on the 'new' button for you to create a new virtual machine, which is the first thing you will do. Then, in the natural operational system, you will have to specify the existence of this machine's files of the service files. You can select Linux for type because it is on top Linux that Kali is built. And for version, Ubuntu 64-bit will be your choice. Though to get Kali up and running on VirtualBox, it is an ideal default setting for us. There is no guarantee it will work perfectly by specifying version and type. Then, the prompt for the amount of memory we want will be the next. You can go for 2GB as even 1GB will still work. Alternatively, you can go ahead and give it as much as you want if you have enough memory.

The hard drive setup is the next step here, which the VirtualBox will ask you. You may choose to use an existing one or create one. So as not to go back and forth between several emulators, you can select VirtualBox Disk Image after selecting the hard drive file type. If you are using VMware, for instance, a more suitable option will be VHD. After that, your storage allocation on the physical hard drive is the next option to choose. Then, you can select dynamic allocation. Next, the amount of allocation for this machine is what you will now choose. You must consider checking how much memory you have available before you go ahead with this action. The place you want to keep your virtual disks can be specified inside VirtualBox. You may then go ahead and hit the 'create' button. But, that is not the end of the process. For us to be sure we can understand them, we may want to play around the main settings. For future reference, you will have the freedom of tackling the virtual environment and this is quite essential. You may want to read more on the topic of virtual machine settings because it is an extensive topic.

You can as well move on to the system settings since, during the creation process, you have covered some items. If you don't have a floppy drive, you can remove floppy under the system. You can prompt VirtualBox to check for any media in the DVD player first in the boot order. It is useful to know that in the initial install, that is the base for our Kali image. If it is necessary, you may want to check that later also, but you can have 2MB for the base memory. As per the above image, ensure that you mirror the extended features. Then, you can boost the memory of the image up to around 128 MB when you move on to 'Display.' Also, in case you want to get naughty with specific graphics, you can have the 3D acceleration enabled. You may run the risk of burning some circuitry and do not give it excessive video memory of you are running on old hardware. After that, you can do one of the most vital settings, which is to check the storage. Ensure that the image file you have downloaded from the official page of Kali Linux is pointing to the empty CD-ROM drive. Also, for you to be given the options to choose your .ISO file, you can achieve that by clicking on the disc icon under attributes.

Now, it is believed that you have mounted the CD-ROM image since the drive represents the .ISO image. You can leave the live DVD/CD checkbox as default and not tick it. You will have to pay attention to the main configuration by checking the settings for the network. Some of them are:

- Generic networking
- Host-only networking
- Internal networking
- Bridged networking
- NAT networking
- Network Address Translation, NAT
- Not attached

You can go to the official page of VirtualBox for you to know more about each mode. And provided your internet connection is wired, this default mode could be enough if all you want to do is to view email inside the guest, download files, and browse the web. As it is for the beginners, you can, for now, use NAT. When you launch the machine, everything should be working well if you are connected via an Ethernet cable. Without an interface card, it may not be possible for you to reach the web in case you don't have a wired connection. Then, you only have to hit on the 'start' to launch the operating system if you intend running Kali in a virtual environment.

Chapter 9: How to Organize Kali Linux

Kali 2.0 was launched by Offensive Security after ten years of evolution. And of all the Kali/Backtrack releases, the easiest to use by far is Kali 2.0. There are some new features with the new Kali if you are used to the original Kali. However, there's nothing better than this! They have streamlined and reorganized the menus completely with a helpful icon representing many of the tools. Here are some new things about Kali 2.0:

- Built-in screencasting
- Desktop notifications
- For faster Metasploit loading, there is a native Ruby 2.0
- New categories and menus
- New user interface

They have streamlined the Kali 2.0 quite well, and compared to earlier versions of Backtrack/Kali; the layout flows quite well. As it is laid out in a concise and clear manner, the feel is that of having everything at your fingertips. To organize your Kali, you can follow the following ways as we examine some of its components.

Overview of the Desktop

Again, everything you will need is at your fingertips on the desktop, which feels and looks quite good.

Apache Webserver

At present, it seems they have removed the Apache web server for restart, start, and stop service icons from Kali 2.0. Well, you may want to use the command below if you want to start them from a terminal prompt:

- To restart – you can use "`/etc/init.d/apache2 restart`' or "service apache2 restart"
- To stop – you can use "`/etc/init.d/apache2 stop`" or "service apache2 stop"
- To start – you can use "`/etc/init.d/apache2 start`" or "service apache2 start"

You will notice the change from Kali 1 concerning the default webpage as you can now surf the webserver of Kali. Now, located in a folder called HTTP, there is one level deeper for the root website as well. As such, instead of the old directory "/var/www/," you can now drop the folders or pages of your website into the directory "/var/www/html/" when you use the Apache server.

Screencasting

You can now use screencasting because there is a built-in screencasting feature in Kali 2.0. You have the ability to record in real-time the adventures of your security testing.

Places Menu

Within your Kali, you have links to various locations contained in the Places menu.

Workspaces

There are also workspaces in the earlier versions of Backtrack/Linux. Workspace is the additional desktop screens that you can use in case you don't know the workspace. For all the windows that you have opened, you can get an overview of them using the 'super key.' Also, you can open the workspace menu if you have a touch-screen monitor. Between the workspaces, you will have the ability of dragging and dropping specific running programs.

Auto-Minimizing Windows

At times, some windows disappear or auto-minimize, which is another thing in the new Kali 2.0. On the favorite bar, to the left of the associated icon, you will see a white circle when a window is minimized. The first terminal window will appear if you click on the terminal icon once, and both minimized terminal windows will reappear when you click it twice. Also, to see minimized windows, you can press "Alt-tab." Then, to see additional windows, you can arrow around when you have the "alt-tab" pressed.

Command-Line Tools

It is in the directory "/usr/share that they have the majority of tools installed. When you type the names of these tools in a terminal, you can run these tools and also other tools in the menu. For you to familiarize yourself with both the share directory and the menu system, you may want to take a few moments on that.

Application Menu

Under the Application menu, you will see the location of a list of common program favorites. And by type, there is a logical layout of the tools. For example, if you want to see the most common web app testing tools, all you have to do is click on the Web Application Analysis menu item. You will see a list of all of the tools for a specific category. It is due to the fact the top tools are shown by the menu system, and in Kali, not all of the tools are available. Essentially, available in the menu system of Kali are only a fraction of the installed tools and it is only from the command-line that most of the tools can be available.

Favorites Bar

On the desktop's left side, you will see a customizable "Favorite bar" in the new Kali. With this, you can get into the action quickly since you can get the applications you use most time with this menu list. Through the required dependencies, you can start the represented tool automatically with just a click. For example, before you launch Metasploit, if you want to be sure you have created the default database, you can prestart the database software by clicking on the button for Metasploit. Then, you can see various applications on the bottom of the favorites bar by clicking on the "show applications." In folders, you can arrange the programs by type. You can also use the search bar by typing what you want if you don't see the app you are looking for.

Chapter 10: Scanning (nmap, massscan, hping3) and Managing Networks (Wireshark)

During the course of penetration testing, a very essential host detector and network scanning tool are network mapped, nmap. Mainly, they use nmap as a security scanner and vulnerability detector which makes it a powerful utility as well as using it to enumerate and gather information. Since it can run on several different operating systems such as Mac, BSD, Linux, and Windows, this makes nmap a multipurpose tool. They use nmap for several powerful purposes including:

- Securing holes and detecting the vulnerability, such as nmap scripts
- Operating system detection, software version, and hardware address

- It works for service discovery, that is, detecting the version and software to the respective port
- Port enumeration and discovery; detecting ports that are open on the host
- Host discovery; detecting the live host on the network

As a common tool, nmap is available for both the graphical user interface and command-line interface. And to perform scanning, nmap utilizes several methods, some of which are FTP bounce scanning, TCP reverse ident scanning, TCP connect() scanning, and many more.

Effective Use of nmap

Since we have a difference between an advance scanning and basic, simple scanning, the target machine has a huge dependence on the usage of nmap. For us to get the right outcome by bypassing the intrusion preventive/detection software and firewall, there is a need to make use of advanced techniques. You will see some examples below of a few basic commands their usage:

On the target system, if you intend to scan a specific port, such as scanning only on the target computer Telnet, FTP, and HTTP, then you will need relevant parameter to use the nmap command. Also, you may as well call the file in the exclude parameter if the lists of IP addresses that you intend to exclude are contained in a file that you have. Another scenario is that since it tends to be dangerous for you, you may want to exclude specific IP addresses if you want to scan the entire subnet. As such, use the excluding parameter when you use the nmap command. You will need to add an `-sL` parameter to the command if you intend to see the entire list of the hosts that you are scanning.

Enumerating a Huge Quantity of Hosts with Massscan

For a while now, massscan has been around, and all around the world, pentesters are making use of it. In a second, masscan can transmit up to 10 million packets as a reconnaissance tool. Massscan utilizes a custom IP/TCP stack and asynchronous transmission with different reception and transmission of packets using different threads.

You can quickly enumerate a vast amount of hosts using massscan. Essentially, massscan can scan the whole internet as quickly as 6 minutes, according to the author of the tool. And because of the high rate of its transmission, they also use massscan for stress testing. For anyone to accomplish those high rates, they will need special drivers like NICs and PF_RING. Since it interacts with the use of similar style of nmap, this part makes it a convenient tool.

Massscan Features

- Custom IP/TCP stack
- Basic vulnerability scanning such as heartbleed
- Banner grabbing
- Nmap style target option and specification
- Nmap style output
- Ultrafast port scanning: up to 10M packets per second in transmission (requiring PF_RING drivers and capable – NIC)

Uses of Masscan

- Random scanning for knowledge or fun
- Internet enumeration
- Enumeration of several subnets within an organization
- Enumeration of a large number of hosts
- For the mapping of the network, massscan can be used as the first recon tool

Hping3 as a Packet Generator and Network Scanning Tool

As a free analyzer and packet generator for the IP/TCP protocol for the Antirez distribution, hping is a network scanning tool. For network security, hping3 is one kind of a tester, and for security testing and auditing of networks and firewalls, it is one of the de facto tools. They also use it for the exploitation of the idle scan scanning method, which now has its implementation in the nmap security scanner. As an analyzer/assembler for IP/TCP packet, a command-line oriented is the network scanning tool hping. Even when hping can do more than sending ICMP echo requests, the ping(8) Unix command inspired the interface. Its features include the ability to send files between a covered channel, possession of a traceroute mode, and support for RAW-IP, ICMP, UDP, and TCP protocols. In the past, they only used hping as a network scanning tool. However, some people use it in several manners to test hosts and networks.

Some of the Usages of hping Network Scanning Tool

- Network scanning tool
- Using Tk interface, it is simple to use networking utilities
- Prototype IDS systems
- Security and networking research in the event of emulating complicated IP/TCP behaviour
- Concept exploits proof
- Automated firewalling tests
- Write real applications related to IP/TCP security and testing
- Learn IP/TCP
- Networking research
- Exploitation of identified vulnerabilities of IP/TCP stacks
- Test IDSes
- Test firewalling rules
- Perform the idle scan (with an easy user interface for implementation in nmap)

- Using the standard utilities network scanning tool to probe/ping/traceroute hosts behind a firewall that blocks attempts
- Students learning IP/TCP can also get adequate knowledge through hping
- Auditing IP/TCP stacks
- Remote uptime guessing
- Remote OS fingerprinting
- Advanced traceroute, under all the supported protocols
- Manual path MTU discovery
- Using fragmentation, TOS, and different protocols for network testing
- Advanced port scanning
- Firewall testing

Securing and Monitoring Your Network with Wireshark

The toolkit for a network security analyst is one of the most powerful tools known as wireshark that people also referred to before as Ethereal. Through a variety of levels, from bits comprising a single packet to information on connection, wireshark can examine the details of traffic as it peers inside the network as a network packet analyzer. Wireshark can troubleshoot security issues in the network of a device and also analyze security events through its depth and flexibility inspection. Since it is free, the price of wireshark is also great!

Wireshark Installation

It is as simple as ABC to install wireshark. For Mac OS X or Windows, you can download the binary versions. Also, for most flavors of Unix/Linux, there's availability of wireshark through the standard software distribution systems. And on other operating systems, the source code is available for installation. For the Windows version, the team that developed wireshark built it on top of the WinPcap packet capture library. And if you don't have WinPcap already in your installation and you are using Windows, you may have to have it installed to run it. Here is a caveat: before you run wireshark installer, you can use the manual process to remove an outdated version of WinPcap through the "Add/Remove Programs" in the control panel. The process of installation is the same with the wizard-based sequence that uses two main prompts: at startup, it will ask if you intend to start the WinPcap Netgroup Packet Filter, NPF service and if you want to have WinPcap installed. For you to capture packets, you can choose the former option that will allow you even if you don't have administrator privileges. It is only administrators that will be able to run wireshark if you have this service enabled.

Chapter 11: Firewalls

Based on a set of security rules, when you intend to block or permit data packets as well as monitor outgoing and incoming network traffic, a network security device that you can use is a firewall. For a firewall to block malicious traffic such as hackers and viruses, you will need to establish a barrier between your incoming traffic and internal network from external sources. You can improve the connection of computer security like the internet or LAN when you use tools like firewalls. An integral part of your network's comprehensive security framework is the firewall. With the use of a code wall that inspects each individual data packet as it arrives, the firewall's either side, both outbound and inbound from the system, to determine whether it can give it access to be blocked or pass, a firewall completely isolates your computer from the Internet.

When it enables granular control over the kinds of system processes and functions that have access to the resources of networking, you can further enhance the security through the capability of firewalls. For it to deny or allow traffic, there are several host conditions and signatures that these firewalls use. You can operate, setup, and install firewalls relatively easily even when they sound complex. The belief of some people is that when they have a firewall installed, the traffic that passes through the network segment will be controlled. However, a firewall that is host-based can be suitable for you. On your computer, you can have them executed, including using it with Internet Connection Firewall, ICF. Fundamentally, there is a similarity to the function of the two firewalls; to stop intrusion and offer a strong technique of access control policy. To put it simply, as access control policy enforcement points, a firewall is a system that safeguards your computer.

Functions of Firewalls

In essence, here are some of the basic functions of firewalls:
- Act as an intermediary
- Report and record events
- Control and manage network traffic
- Validate access
- Defend resources

The Definition of Personal Firewall

In the world of secure computing, it's quite essential for you to understand your need for a firewall. And since it aids our understanding of how a firewall may address those needs, we need to understand the goals of information security.

The Need for Personal Firewall

Electronically, you will connect your computer to a broad network in the times of high-speed Internet access. You will have limited protection or control unless you have installed a personal firewall. There are some drawbacks to any high-speed connection, typical of anything else. Ironically, the same feature that makes a connection with a high-speed vulnerable is the same reason that makes it attractive. In some ways, you may be leaving your front door of your house unlocked and open with your connection to the high-speed internet. Some of the features of high-speed internet connections include:

- Constant active connection – this is the fact that when your computer is connected to the internet every time, it is vulnerable
- Access of high-speed – this means that it can be quite faster for intruders to break into your computer

- A regular IP – it will be easier for an intruder to find your computer again and again after they have discovered you

Using a Personal Firewall for Defense

Compared to an ordinary 56Kbps connection, now it is clear to you how, when you are online on a high-speed internet connection, you are vulnerable. Now, the threat posed by this type of connection is now known to you, and how you can defend yourself against it is what you need to know. Here are some of the vital reasons for a personal firewall:

- You can easily develop policies for security to suit your individual needs since most personal firewalls are highly configurable
- When your computer's program tries to connect to the internet, you wish to be kept informed
- The home network that you run requires you to keep it isolated from the internet
- You use a public WiFi network when you connect to the internet in an airport, café, or park
- With an 'always on' broadband connection, you surf the internet at home

Firewalls Types

Though the two are suitable, you can have firewalls as hardware or software. With port applications and numbers, you can regulate traffic through the installation of a software firewall program on your computer while you can install the hardware firewall type between the gateway and your network. The most common firewall type is the packet-filtering firewalls, and in case they don't match an established security rule set, they prevent packets from passing through after they have examined them. The purpose of these firewall types is to analyze the destination and source of the packets for IP addresses. It will thus be trusted to enter the network if the packets match those of an 'allowed' rule on the firewall.

Stateless and stateful are the two categories of the packet-filtering firewalls. The ones that are easy targets for hackers are the stateless firewalls since they lack context by examining packets independently of one another. On the other hand, stateful firewalls tend to be much more secure because they remember information about previously passed packets. Though packet-filtering firewalls ultimately offer quite basic protection and tend to be quite inadequate, they can be indeed effective. For example, for them to determine the adverse effect of the application that the content of the requests is reaching can be quite hard for them. Thus, there will be no way for the firewall to know when there could be a deletion of a database from a misconceived trusted source if it allows a malicious request. Those that are equipped to detect such threats are the proxy and next-generation firewalls.

SMLI, Stateful Multilayer Inspection Firewalls

While these firewalls compare them against trusted packets, they filter packets at the application, transport, and network layers. Also, if they pass the layer individually, SMLI only allows them to pass after they examined the entire packet, which is typical of NGFW firewalls. They ensure the potential of all initiated communications happening only with trusted sources as they determine the state of the communication and also by examining the packets.

NAT, Network Address Translation Firewalls

These firewalls keep individual IP address hidden when they use a single IP address to connect to the internet by allowing several devices with independent network addresses. As such, they offer greater security against attacks because attackers can't capture specific details when they are scanning a network for IP addresses. These firewalls are rooted between outside traffic and a group of computers with proxy firewalls having similarities with NAT firewalls.

Proxy Firewalls

At the level of application, these firewalls have the network filtered. They are planted between two end systems, which are not like the basic firewalls. The firewall must receive a request from the client and using a set of security for the evaluation, and after that, keep it blocked or give permission. Essentially, layer 7 protocols like FTP and HTTP are monitored by proxy firewalls and for them to detect malicious traffic, they utilize both deep packet and stateful inspections.

NGFW, Next-Generation Firewalls

These firewalls blend additional functionality with the technology of traditional firewall like anti-virus, intrusion prevention systems, encrypted traffic inspection, and many more. Essentially, it has the inclusion of DPI, deep packet inspection. It is within the packet itself that deep packet inspection examines the data while looking at packet headers is what basic firewalls only look. With this process, users can stop, categorize, and identify packets effectively with malicious data.

Chapter 12: Obtaining User Information: Maltego, Scraping, Shodan/Censys.io

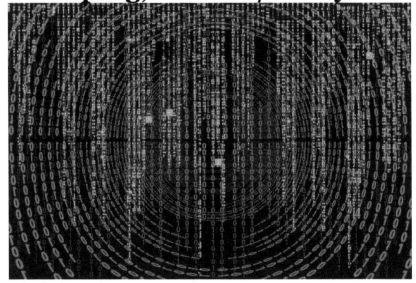

Maltego reveals how information is connected to each other as a forensic and open-source application. The relationship between several information types can aid in identifying the unknown relationship as well as giving a better picture of their links. When you use maltego, you will have the ability to find relationships and also the people's link, such as mutual friends, social profiles, websites, and companies with the gathered information relationships. You may want to gather the connection between net blocks, DNS names, and domains if you intend to gather information regarding any infrastructure.

Architecture of Maltego

Seed servers receive the request from the maltego client over HTTPS in XML format. Then, it is the TAS servers that will take the request from the seed server before the service provider then get the request. The maltego client will then get the results of the request. For more privacy, you may want to consider having your TAS servers. At present, the basic and professional modules are the two types of maltego, and the availability of the modules are the two major differences between both servers. CTAS is what the basic server has while in the professional server, you will see the PTTAS, SQLTAS, and CTAS.

From within maltego, you can perform several pentesting related tasks with PTTAS, including banner grabbing, port scan, and so on. Also, accessing SQL database is possible for TAS through SQLTAS. You can also get results after performing numerous SQL queries using this module. Postgress, Oracle, DB2, MSSQL, and MySQL are some of the supported types. Then, available in public sever are the transforms that are contained in the commercial TAS.

Launching Maltego

For anyone to start maltego, you will go to the applications and look for backtrack. From there, you will get the information gathering and then to the network analysis where you will then see DNS analysis. From there, you will get into maltego. You will be prompted to register your product if you are accessing it for the first time. You will only need to input your email address and password if you have registered an account already. It will update the transforms when you have validated your login.

Hit on the tab 'investigate' after the updates of the transforms, and from the palette; you can choose your desired option. In the palette, you will see two major categories, which are personal and infrastructure. Also, other entities can be imported into the palette, for example, the Shodan entity. With the aid of their banner, you can find specific switches, routers, servers, and so on through a search engine like Shodan.

Web Scraping with Python

Let's assume you want to quickly pull a huge quantity of data from websites as fast as possible, how can you accomplish this feat without getting your data by going to each website at a time? Well, the short answer is web scraping. For what you intend to do to be faster and easier, you may want to result to web scraping. If you want to collect data from websites and when the volume is huge, you can use web scraping. However, what can instigate someone to want to collect massive data from sites? It is essential to discuss the web scraping application for us to understand the reason:

- **Job listings**: some details from websites regarding interviews, job openings, and so on, which users can easily access since it is listed in one place.
- **Development and research:** they collect temperature, general information, statistics, and so on from websites, which are a large set of information by using web scraping, and they use the result for R&D or to carry out surveys after analyzing it.
- **Social media scraping:** finding out what is trending by collecting data from social media websites like Twitter through web scraping.
- **Gathering email address:** web scraping is used by several organizations that use email marketing to send bulk emails after collecting them.
- **Price comparison:** for the comparison of the prices of products, web scraping is used by services like ParseHub to obtain information from online shopping sites.

The extraction of a massive quantity of information from websites is a technique of web scraping. The website's data are not structured, and to have it is a structured form, these unstructured data are collected by web scraping to do the job. Writing code, APIs, and online services are some of the different ways to scrape websites. Web scraping is allowed by some websites, while others don't allow it if we want to shift to the legal side of it. You may want to look at the "robots.txt" file of the website for you to know if such a website allows web scraping or not. If you want to scrape a website, all you have to do is to append "/robots.txt" to the URL for you to find this file. For example, to see the "robots.txt" file of the website Georgia Movers, the URL will be www.georgiamovers.com/robots.txt.

Shodan and Censys

It is in the Internet of Things that we are now living. Starting from the street security cameras and traffic light management systems to home WiFi routers, things that are connected to the Internet are always in our encounter. And it is both on the web and the real world that we can find all of them because they have a connection. With Google helping to discover your sought-after data on the web, you can also find these connected devices with some special search engines.

Let's welcome Shodan and Censys!

Since it has been in existence for about 7 years now, for the Internet of Things, the foremost, as well as the first search engine, is shodan. The inspiration behind the name came from a highly villainous artificial intelligence named Shodan, who was the System Shock, the computer game series' main antagonist. Though it has the capability of wrecking harm, shodan in the real-world is not as relentless. However, you will want to know how the search engine works before we go on to the bad news.

Shodan is typically similar to someone that knocks on every door that they see as they wander throughout the neighborhood. However, there is the whole world instead of some city or knocking on every IPv4 address. This person would have some information and will give it to you if you ask them about a specific part of the neighborhood or a specific type of doors. The person would tell you the number of the doors, the individuals who answer these doors, and their utterances. And about those Internet of Things, you can get their information from shodan, which includes whether there is a web interface you can use, their type, and how they are called. Through, relatively cheap, you will need to subscribe to you to use shodan because it is not completely free.

Except there are no locks on some doors, you may find nothing so weird about knocking on some doors. And for the bad guys to break in, it may not be possible for anyone. Some systems that use default passwords and logins, including IP cameras and unprotected routers, are the representations of these doors in the world of Internet of things. You will see yourself gaining complete access to the password and login when you have managed to figure out them after entering their web-interface. And because you can easily find these default information about passwords and logins on the manufacturers' website, everything is no longer rocket science. And if it has the support of an IP camera, you can control and even see everything if it is an IP camera. Also, you may alter the settings if it is a router. You can even use a scary voice to talk to the poor baby if it is a baby monitor. Everything is up to the standards of your morals.

Chapter 13: Kali Linux on Portable Devices Like Raspberry Pi

Though, it can be fun enough to test networks, spoof accounts, or crack WiFi passwords. However, you may need an easily portable rig if you intend to take the show on the road. And so, here come the Raspberry Pi and Kali Linux. They designed Kali Linux for network penetration testing as an operating system. For you to test for Bluetooth vulnerabilities, spoof networks, WiFi passwords cracking, and plenty of other things, you have the chance of running it on your laptop. You need to know that you can be charged with a felony and get yourself arrested for violating the Computer Security Act if you break into protected networks using this knowledge. You can only use this knowledge to play with networks you control, for your learning, or simply use it for good. Now, since we have talked extensively about Kali Linux, and for the sake of not repeating all that you have read before, our focus will be on how we will build our Raspberry Pi and the version we will use. So, let's get it done!

For you to use Raspberry Pi, they don't require a lot of power for you to use them as a credit sized, small computer. You will have a super-portable system testing device that you can easily take with you anywhere you go with the combination of Kali Linux and Raspberry Pi.

The Essentials

- For you to perform initial installation, you will need a desktop computer
- Get a portable, small wireless keyboard with touchpad that one side of a small bag can contain
- It tends to be quite useful if you are carrying the Raspberry Pi with you around. So, a case is fine but optional
- New version of point-to-this-screen is essential though with Raspberry Pi 2 or newer versions; it doesn't fit flush
- An 8 GB SD card
- A Wi-Fi card
- You will be fine with a few external 5V batteries that use a USB part built for smartphones. So, you need a pack of battery
- Model 2 or B/B+ of Raspberry Pi. Though to install Raspberry Pi 2, you will need some additional steps; you may want to use the Model B+ if you don't wish to go through those steps.
-

Step 1: Installation of Kali on the Raspberry Pi

For the Raspberry Pi, downloading and installing the touch screen build for Kali Linux will be the first thing you will need to do. The installation process is quite typical of installing any other operating system for Raspberry Pi. Here is a quick way to go about it:

Installation of Kali to Windows SD Card

1. For your hardware, you will need to download the Kali Linux Raspberry Pi. You can grab the Pi 2 version for Raspberry Pi 2 and the TFT version for model B/B++. Inside it, you will unzip the img file. You will need to take note here because, for Raspberry Pi, you will have to download the standard version of Kali Linux if you're not using the touch screen display.
2. You will need to have the application (.exec file) unzipped within after downloading Win32DiskImager.
3. With the use of a card reader, you will then have your SD card inserted into the Windows computer.
4. Then, you will double-click on the application, Win32DiskImager.exe that you have just downloaded.
5. At the top right of the device, you will click on the drop-down menu to select from the list if the application doesn't automatically detect your SD card.
6. The Raspbian .img file that you have just downloaded can be found when you click on the folder icon of the file from the application's image section.
7. Win32DiskImager will work its magic as you wait for it after you have clicked the 'write' button. You can insert

your card into your Raspberry Pi after you have safely ejected your SD card when it finishes.

Kali installation in OS X SD Card

1. For you to work with it on your hardware, you will firstly need to have Kali Linux Raspberry Pi image downloaded. You will take Pi 2 version for Raspberry Pi 2 and TFT version for model B/B++. The standard version of Kali Linux for the Raspberry Pi is essential to be downloaded if it is the screen display that you are using.

2. For your installed version of OS X, have the appropriate version selected as you unzip the application after you have downloaded RPi-sd card builder.

3. With the use of a card reader, have your SD card inserted into your Mac.

4. Then, you can have your RPi-sd card builder opened. There will be an instant prompt for you to select an image of Raspbian. The file that you have had downloaded earlier is all you will have to select.

5. Then, another prompt will inquire about the connection of your SD card. All that is required of you is to click on 'continue' since it is connected when you inserted it earlier. Then, the options for SD card will be presented to you. It will be checked, and you won't see anything else on the list if you have only had one inserted. Click ok on the card you want to use if not.

6. Then, you will enter the password for administration and press enter.

7. If there is any ejection of the SD card, you will see yet another prompt. Since for the application to perform a direct copy, it needs to unmount; there's nothing weird

about it. In the Finder, for your SD card not to be available any longer, you will need to double-click it. A word of caution here: NEVER remove it from your USB port. You can click continue when you are sure.

8. Your SD card prepping will finish by the RPi-sd card builder. Then, you can insert it into your Raspberry Pi unit after you have safely ejected it.

Step 2: the Display Hook-Up

The touch screen works perfectly with the general-purpose input/output, which the Raspberry Pi has. You will see how this works ideally because, in the corner, it is the set of pins on your Raspberry Pi. Click into the display of the Raspberry Pi.

Step 3: Have Everything Plugged in and Launch

At this stage, you will need to plug in everything through the attacked display. Have your Wi-Fi adapter plugged into the USB ports. After that, plug the Pi into your pack of batteries. Here, you can experience a clunky and slow process for the startup. If it takes some time, don't panic. First, before the startup process of the boot, for a bit while, you will see a white screen. Finally, a login screen will greet you. For you to get your screen working, you may have to work through some form of setup if you are using a Raspberry Pi 2. You may simply have to go to the next step if it is the B+ that you are using. Mainly, to get the screen running, there may be some needed steps for the current Raspberry Pi 2. A white, sad screen will welcome you when you boot it up initially. However, getting the screen working is not too hard. Unfortunately, Pi attachment may not require an HDMI monitor or through this part, you may need access into SSH. Then, to boot up your Pi, simply connect either of those.

Step 4: Enable Wi-Fi as you Log in

For you to make use of the tools within Kali Linux, you will want to enable the Wi-Fi card as you log in. your Wi-Fi card will be recognized automatically by the Raspberry Pi. However, it is essential to get into your network. The user interface of Kali Linux then needs to be powered up in the first place. Finally, you must change your device's password before you engage in anything else. If you don't, your device can be controlled by another person with the hacking skills.

Chapter 14: MalDuino

MalDuino has the capabilities of keyboard injection as an arduino-powered USB device. At superhuman speed, MalDuino will act as a typing, keyboard commands when you power it. Anything is possible with MalDuino since you can alter the desktop wallpaper or gain a reverse shell. Also, MalDuino can work well for pranksters, hobbyists, and penetration testers. The best BadUSB experience is all that MalDuino aims to provide. And using open-source libraries, it is through the arduino IDE that they have MalDuino programmed when it comes to software. You can convert the script written in DuckyScript into the code MalDuino will understand. For them to program it simply like, they would an Arduino; this makes it possible for expert arduino tinkerers to program it as well as making it newbie-friendly. The two versions of MalDuino are Lite and Elite.

Elite

You can select the script you intend running from the card since this version has four DIP switches and a Micro-SD card reader, and it is quite bigger. Also, you can program the keystroke injection scripts that the Micro-SD card stored apart from burning the fireware only once. This process is in contrary to the Lite version, which, when you want to run a different script, it will need to be flashed. You can drop, repurpose, or reprogram all these features altogether because it is straight from the Arduino that they programmed the two MalDuinos. Although you may have a few pins to play around with, you can purchase one and simply prefer to use it as a usual Arduino. You will be prompted to participate in the crowd-funding campaign particularly with the freedom that it offers.

Lite

The Lite version contains a switch apart from the USB connector, and this version is quite small. You can choose between programming and running mode with the function of the switch and the indication that the script has finished running through a LED. With more than enough space for most scripts, on its 32KB of onboard memory, the Lite stores a script. You can use the script converter to convert the scripts to malduino-friendly code since you can use a text editor to write scripts. Then, with the Arduino IDE, you can as well upload a script. Using the switch at the back, you can toggle the Lite into ready mode after you have unplugged the MalDuino Lite. Then, you can start using it!

The Hardware

The board of the Elite version measures around 4.6 cm x 1.1 cm, roughly 1.8 in x 0.43 in, which you can use an old case for it. For the Micro-SD card and DIP switches, you may need to cut some holes for them. It may come to your realization that the firmware it ships with is likely some kind of QC test for the dips after you exercise some RTFM and play around with the switches. Depending on which switches are on, these features make the output of MalDuino the numbers 1 to 4.

The Setup

Your Arduino IDE must not only be installed but also up to date when you want to set up the MalDuino. Because they programmed the Elite as a 'Sparkfun Pro Micro" that runs at 8 MHz and 3.3 V, it will be required of you to install the Sparkfun boards and open up the board manager. Then, the online portal of the Malduino Script Converter is your next point to go since there so many purposes that it servers like:

- For you to import to the IDE, it auto-generates the Arduino project
- You will have the freedom of selecting the language of your keyboard layout
- Between the Elite and Lite version, you can convert scripts through it

You only need to have the MalDuino flashed once and then store new scripts using the Micro-SD card when it is in normal operation as you empty script to download the project or create a simple script for the Elite version.

The Software

For you to run a command, a quick shortcut will be the combination of the ALT-F2 since you are running Linux. As such, you can save a file to `1111.txt` after scripting that into a file. Then, for a file that corresponds to the recent dip switch state, the search will be on the Elite for the Micro-SD card if you power the dip switch 4 and 2. As such, there will be an attempt by the software on parsing the content and finding the file with the name 0101.txt, i.e., not the binary representation of the number 4 and 2 but in dip switch order 1,2,3, and 4. Then, there will be a quick flashing of the red LED when it finishes. It is possible that only command functioning accurately is the ALT-F2 combo, and nearly all commands worked. Thus, you won't get any run command window without ALT-F2.

Protecting Yourself From MalDuino

As keystroke injection tools, a wider family of USB devices, referred to as BadUSBs is MalDuino. They have the capability of doing several types of devilish things by taking advantage of keyboard input as a trusted method of interfacing with a computer. However, what are the measures you can take to guard yourself against MalDuino? You can mitigate or protect yourself from the dangers of BadUSB attacks with the following 3 ways:

Admin Rights Lockdown

It doesn't matter if you are concerned about BadUSB attack or you are not; doing this can be quite useful. If you want to make changes to the admin-level, you only have to provide the prompt of yes or no to make changes that require admin rights on Windows 10. Even if the person is the admin, you will see that it is wrong and silly to provide someone that level of control. Before handling the keys to the castle, you can change this with a registry level edit to make the operating system require your admin password.

Duckhunt

This technique is applicable on Windows. There is a small application on github that can run as a backdoor process. The rate at which your keys are typed is what it continually monitors. When it detects unusual typing speeds, it will block all HID. However, some of the first few characters of an attach can likely get through and that is the only downside of it.

Physical Protection

It is simply a catch-all solution, and it is quite vital not to allow unauthorized devices from being plugged into your system. You can invest in some port blocker devices to block all access to USB ports physically. You may have to look deeper in the case of critical infrastructure. All the same, you can prevent any attack by using it when you are out in public.

Chapter 15: Kismet

As a wireless intrusion detection framework, kismet is a wardriving tool, sniffer, device detector, and wireless network. While kismet functions in compliance with hardware such as RTLSDR as well as some specialized capture hardware, it also works with certain software-defined radio, Bluetooth interfaces, and Wi-Fi interfaces. To some extent and under the WSL framework, kismet also functions with Windows but works well with OS X and Linux. Kismet works with Bluetooth and Wi-Fi interfaces, as well as other hardware devices on Linux. The built-in Wi-Fi interfaces enable it to function on OS X and works with remote captures on Windows 10.

Watching the Activities of Wi-Fi User Using Kismet

With a sight's direct line and directional Wi-Fi antenna, it is possible to detect the signals of Wi-fi passing through the walls of your home, even with its walls of privacy. People can learn a huge amount of data from this information, such as nearby devices' manufacturers, the movements of the residents, and also the network they use at a given time. For fixed targets, using kismet in a fixed situation can result in more nuanced information. Thus, it is ideal at displaying relationships between devices over time instead of just looking for the access point out there. The draw is from signal intelligence methods when we spy on users using kismet, whereby it is through the signals it conveys that we hope to learn about what we can't see. Here, Wi-Fi is the things we are dealing with and the devices that someone owns, human activity, connected devices, and routers are the things we are trying to see. Doing this goes a long way to your imagination. You will be more inclined to put off your Wi-Fi on unused devices and make a switch to a wired network if you are able to figure out that someone could see whether you were using your laptop or on your PlayStation and whether you were in your house. Using a wireless network, they use kismet to scan every available Wi-Fi channels silently by putting it in monitor mode for wireless packets for it to work its magic. You can see automated beacon frames as these packets that can be broadcasted by the wireless APs several times in a second. Also, not yet connected probe frames and data packets exchanged from connected devices. Kismet has the ability to visualize the activity of devices associated with specific networks as well as the networks themselves.

What We Can Get From Wi-Fi

So, how do we manage this situation? You can get on to explore nuanced details about a network you want to watch when you have identified it. You may want to look for details such as the network connection of the hardware and electronics of someone or an organization. You will be able to know the kind of configuration for some devices and also the recognition of various setups types for fingerprint. Not only will laptops and smartphones be plain to you, but you will also have the ability to see connected hydroponics or 3D printers with a setup such as this.

Now, the kind of person you are has a lot of dependence on the usefulness of this information. It would be useful to a thief who wants to discover expensive electronics by snooping around all homes in wireless range. Using a jamming attack, you can potentially target one or avoid one completely because wireless security cameras can be detected by kismet. And when no one is in the house, we can easily infer since it's quite possible for us to see when the devices of clients use data, disappear, and appear. Also, with the use of the Wi-Fi signal data, hackers can combine data of the GPS by wardriving around a neighborhood. Doing this, each address of the wireless network will be possible for hackers when they build a map. Essentially, as there are already mapped networks by Google and Wigle Wifi, there could be an existence of this data. In the neighborhoods, for the detection of suspicious wireless activity, people can also use it as a neighborhood watch.

Essential Tools

There are some things needs to adhere to this guide. You will need kismet for you to run a Linux system, and for the scanning, you will also need a wireless network adapter that is compatible with Kali. Here, the older version which is stable is what we will discuss even though different wireless cards like macOS can run on the recent type of kismet. If your desire is to have it run on the Raspberry Pi, kismet will function perfectly on a Kali-Pi installation as well as a virtual machine.

Step 1: kismet installation:

The git repository will have to undergo a cloning process before the installation of kismet on Kali Linux. You may not need to worry about any dependencies based on the type of operating system that you are using. However, the slightly longer list of dependencies for kismet may be needed to be installed for smooth running of kismet. Since you will have to sort, login, decode, and detect a huge number of wireless data, they are quite needed. Also, you will need to install lots of libraries because you will be controlling a wireless card. Then, you will need to have the installation configured by navigating to the kismet directory. For your specific operating system distribution, this process will have the installation configured. Then, you can create the installation after the completion of that process. You will use the *suidinstall* option to complete the installation by running the resulting file with it. Then, you will install kismet. After the installation, you will need to capture packets as a non-root user by adding yourself to the kismet group. Ensure that your actual username is replaced in the space for "YourUsername."

Step 2: monitor-mode your wireless card:

With the USB settings, you will attach your wireless network card to the virtual machine or to your computer. The commands *ifconfig* or *ip a* can be used to find your card. You can use a "wlan0" or "wlan1" to name your card. You can then put your care in a monitor mode after naming it. At the end of the card's name, you will see a "mon" as it is renamed with this process. And to launch kismet, you will use this name.

Step 3: launch kismet:

It is simple to begin using kismet. For your card that you have put in wireless monitor mode, ensure to put the term after the −c since to specify the source it captures, kismet makes use of the −c. Then, kismet will start capturing packets after starting up. Then, you can return to the menu and make some customizations.

Several Wi-Fi devices that you can detect nearby will appear before you as you start kismet. Based on whether you are using 5 GHz, 2.4 GHz, or the two of them, you will have variance in the number of devices that you can detect.

Chapter 16: Bypassing a Hidden SSH

Now we need to take some time to look at going through and bypassing one of the SSH logins. We are going to do this by adding our own key to a remote server and then getting the access that we want. So if we want to go through and setup the SSH keys so that we can quickly and efficiently log in without a password, we are able to do this with a single command. This is going to be a simple process to go through.

The SSH is going to be known as the Secure Shell, and it is going to be a cryptographic network protocol that is going to be useful for helping us to operate the network services securely over a network that is unsecured. The typical applications that we are going to see with this one are going to include options like logging in with the command line and remote command execution, but it is possible that any network that you want to use is going to be secured with the SSH protocol.

The first step in this process is to make sure that we have been able to run the keygen command in order to generate the keys.

If you have already generated some of these keys, then we are able to skip these steps. The code that we are able to use for this one is below

ssh -keygen -t rsa

Then we are able to go through and use this particular command in order to push the key so that it becomes connected to the remote server. This is going to be something that we are able to modify in order to match the user name of the server and the host name of your server as well. We will be able to go through and use the code below to make this happen.

cat ~/.ssh/id_rsa.pub | ssh user@hostname 'cat >> .ssh/authorized_keys'

The first time that we copy over these keys, we are going to need to enter the password to help the program get set up and ready to go. After that first time, though, we should be able to login without needing a password, or even use the rsync or scp without entering the password at all. You are able to test this iwt the following command:

ssh user@hostname

It is definitely going to be a lot easier to go through compared to typing in a password all of the time.

Nd, that is all that we need to do. It is going to spend some time helping us to get onto the SSH and will make it easier for us to get onto this without needing to use a password each time that we do the work. Getting this done can be hard, and you do need to know the password the first time around, but if you are able to get ahold of this, and you will be able to get onto the network any time that you would like.

Chapter 17: Bypassing a Mac Address Authentication and Open Authentication

Another thing that we are able to do when it comes to hacking is to bypass the Mac Address Authentication in order to get onto the network that we want to use. This is going to be a feature that we are going to find with Mac addresses that will allow us to get onto the system and use it in the manner that we would like. This will ensure that we are able to either get onto our network when it is not working well or on another option that we would like to use, such as hacking into another computer. Let's take a look at how this is going to work.

The Media Access Control address, or the MAC address, is going to be interesting because it is able to uniquely identify each node that is going to show up in a network. It is going to take the form of six pairs of hexadecimal digits, which can include 0 to 9, and all of the letters A to F, that are going to be separated out by either dashes or colons.

This MAC address is usually going to be associated with the network adaptor or a device that has some networking capabilities. Because of this reason, it is going to be known in many cases as the physical address. The first three pairs of these digits in the address are going to be called the Organizational Unique Identifier, and we need to take some time to look at them because they help us to identify the company that either sold or manufactured the device. Then the last three pairs of digits that are going to show up are going to be the specific numbers that just go to that device, and can be like the serial number of the whole process.

With this in mind, we are going to spend some time going through and looking at some of the steps that we need to use in order to bypass the MAC address filtering on some of our wireless networks. The first step that we need to work with is considering that we are going to working with a router that has the MAC Filtering Configured in the first place. We can say that our MAC address is going to be AA-BB-OO-11-22. This is one that is allowed to show up when we are using the MAC filtering on our own wireless network.

Then it is time to move on. We can log into the machine that we are using for Kali Linux and then put that Wi-Fi adapter into the mode that allows it to monitor what is going on around it. This is going to be done with the airmon-ng and can be done with the simple command into our terminal below:

Airmon-ng start wlan()

Now it is possible that some of the processes with Kali Linux when you do this will show us some errors. If you do end up with some issues or an error message here, then you need to kill the process in this program that seems to be having the issue. You are able to do this with the command below:

Kill [pid]

Now it is time to go through and launch another part of this process, which is the Airodum-ng. This will help us to locate the wireless network that we want to work with, and will even help us to see which clients are connected in this whole process. The command that we are able to use to make this one happen is below:

airodump-ng –c [channel] –bssid [target router MAC Address] –i wlanomon

This should then show us a whole list of the clients who are connected to this device at the bottom of our terminal. Then the second column is going to list the MAC addresses of all the connected clients we will be able to spoof at this time in order to get that wireless networked authenticated so we can do what we would like on it.

The one thing to note at this time is that you are only going to get a list with this step if there is actually someone who is connected to the wireless network that we are looking at. If you do not have someone currently connected to the device, then you will not get a list at this point.

Now it is time for us to go on to the next step. After having been able to go through and find the MAC address that you want to use, it is time to go through the process of using the MacChange rin order to spoof the MAC address that we want to work with. We are going to spend our time spoofing the MAC address of your wireless adapter, but the first thing that we need to do here before we get started, we need to take down the interface for monitoring known as wlanomon and wlano. This is going to allow us to make some of the changes that we want to the MAC address. We are able to do this with the following command to make things a little easier:

Airmon-ng stop wlanomon

When that process is done, we are able to take down the wireless interface who's MAC address we want to spoof in the following command:

Ifconfig wlano down

Then this is going to bring us the MacChanger. We are able to use this tool in order to change up the MAC address. The code that we are able to do with this one will be below:

Macchanger -m [New MAC Address] wlano

And then we want to go through and bring all of that back up. Remember, a few steps above, we went through and closed down the system so that we could change ours and get ourselves on this option. But now we want to go through and bring it all back up again. The code that we are able to work with here will include:

Ifconfig wlano up

Now that we have been able to change up the MAC address that is on our wireless adapter to a white listed MAC address that the other network will allow, we are able to try out authenticating with the network and see whether this worked and if we are able to connect to the process as well.

And that is all there is to get this done. Keep in mind that this process can take a bit of time if you are not going to find someone who is on the network right in the beginning. You may need to have some patience with this one to make sure that it is going to work the way that you would like and to ensure that you can actually find the right MAC address that is going to work with that router.

But once you have been able to go through and change up your MAC address so that it works well with one of the other options that belong to that wireless network so that you are able to get on as well. This is a simple process is going to be able to help us learn more about the process and how we are able to work with getting onto the network that we would like along the way.

Chapter 18: Hacking WPA and WPA2

The world of wireless networks is going to be great for a lot of consumers. It adds on a lot of protection to the networks of the past, and it is going to be important to helping us to work with our wireless network while on the move and without having to be connected to your cable all of the time. The WPA and WPA2 options are going to be some of the best when it comes to keeping your information safe, but it is possible for hackers to get onto them if they are patient, and they are ready to go through and take on the hard work. That is why we are going to spend some time in this chapter taking a look at the steps that are necessary to hack onto these two wireless networks.

The first thing that we need to take a look at is preparing our attack. We need to first have a better understanding of when we are able to legally hack into a Wi-Fi network. In most regions, the only time that you are able to legally hack onto some of these networks is when the network belongs to you, or if it belongs to someone who has given us written permission to hack into the network so that you can check it and make sure that it is safe from a hacker. Hacking networks that don't meet the criteria that are above, then the hacking process is illegal and it could be known as a federal crime if you are caught in the act.

Now that this is out of the way, it is time for us to go through and download the disk image of Kali Linux. This is going to be one of the preferred tools to work with when it is time to hack these networks. You can download the installation image, also known as the ISO, by using the following steps:

1. The first step that we will work with is to go to the https://www.kali.org/downloads/ on the web browser of your needs.
2. Click HTTP next to any of the versions of this that you would like to use.
3. Wait for the file to finish with the downloading process.

From here, we want to be able to attach a flash drive over to the computer that we are working with. The flash drive that we are using is required to come with 4 gigabytes of space or higher in order to complete this process. Then we can make the flash drive bootabe. Finish up the rest of the steps that you need to do to get the Kali Linux system set up and ready to go on your own computer.

When the Kali Linux system is set up and ready, it is time to begin the actual hack that we want to accomplish. We can do this by opening up the terminal for Kali Linux on your computer. You can find and click on this Terminal app icon, which is going to look like a black box that has a white ">_" on it. You can also just click on Alt, Ctrl, T to open this terminal up.

This is the time where you will want to install Aircrack to help with the attack. You are able to type in the command that is below to help you get this one started:

sudo apt-get install aircrack-ng

When the prompt comes up for this one, you will want to enter in the password. You can type in the password you use to log into that computer in the first place. Then press on the Enter button. This is going to make sure that the root access is going to be enabled for any of the other commands that you would like to be able to execute in the Terminal. If you decide at this time to open up another window for a Terminal, which is possible, remember that you may have to go through and run a command with the sudo prefix or choose to enter the password into the system again to get the best results.

This is where we are going to be able to install the Aircrack-ng program that we were talking about before. When it prompts you to, you should press on Y, then wait until the program has time to finish installing overall. When this installation is done, it is time to turn on the airmon-ng. type in the command to do this and then press on Enter to continue.

Then it is time for us to go through and find the name of the monitor that we want to use. You are going to find this located somewhere in the Interface column. If you are working to do this attack on your own network, then it is going to be named as wlan0. If you do not see the name of the monitor at all, then be aware that your specific card for Wi-Fi is not going to support this kind of monitoring at all.

Now it is time for us to go through and start the process of monitoring our network. You are able to do this with the following command below, and then press enter when you are done

Airmon-ng start wlan0.

Make sure that you press the right name of the network that you would like to monitor. If you are doing your own, then you would add in the wlano. But if you are trying to monitor the wireless of another computer, then you will need to make some changes in order to handle this and make sure that you are actually managing the different network that you would like.

Then we need to go through and enable a monitor mode interface with this. When we find that, we are able to enter the following command to help us get this set up:

Iwconfig

Now, there could be a few different processes that show up, and it is possible that some of them are going to return errors to us. If this happens, then we will want to kill any of the processes that are going to return errors to us. This is often going to happen when the Wi-Fi card is going to conflict with some of the running services on your computer. You are able to kill these processes when you go through and use the command below:

Airmon-ng check kill

While we are here, we want to review the name of the monitor interface. In most cases, the name is going to be something that is pretty simple, like mono or wlanomon. We also want to make sure to tell the computer that it is time to listen to some of the nearby routers. To get a list of the routers that happen to be in the same range as you, you are able to enter the command below:

Airodump-ng mono

Make that you replace the mono with the right part. We want to have it filled in as the name of the monitor interface that we used in the previous step, or this is not going to work the way that we would like.

As you are searching around, we need to make sure that we are doing some searching here. We need to be able to find the router that we would most like to hack. At the end of each string of text that comes your way, you are going to see a name. You want to look through this to find the one that belongs to the network that you would most like to hack into in the process.

During this process, we need to make sure that we are working with the right router, and that we are choosing one that comes with WPA or WPA2 security that is attached back to it. If you see one of these on the left of the name of the network, then it is time to proceed. Otherwise, this is not going to be a network that you are able to hack along the way.

This is where we are going to be able to note the MAC address and the channel number of the router that we want to work with. These are going to be the pieces of information that we should notice on the left of the name of the network. The MAC address is going to be the line of numbers that we are going to find on the far-left side of the line for the router. On the other hand, the channel is going to be a number of some sort that is found to the left of the tag that you have for the WPA or WPA2.

In this part, we are going to be able to monitor the selected network until we see a handshake. This is going to occur when an item connects to a network, or when the computer is able to connect to a router. Enter in the code below in order to make sure that we are replacing the components that are necessary of the command with the information on the network:

Airodum-ng -c channel –bssid MAC -w /root/Desktop/ mono

In this one, there are going to be a few things that are going to happen. First, we are able to replace the channel with the channel number that we were able to find in the other step. Then we want to replace MAC with the MAC address that we plan to us or spy on here.

Remember that we also need to go through and replace the mono with whatever the name of the interface is that you want to work with.

When this is all in place, we just wait around for some time to see that handshake appears. Once you see a line that has the tag of WPA handshake, and it is followed with a MAC address that shows up at the top of your screen on the right, then it is time to proceed. It is also possible for us to move this along and not wait around all of the time, it is possible for us to force a handshake using the deauth attack before we continue on with this part.

When it is time to go through and get that handshake, then you will be able to get onto the network and look at what is going on, as long as the other person does not have the proper security on their network at that time. You will then be able to get through some of the security protocols that are there, and this allows you to look around, read through and change some of the packets that are shown, and so much more. You need to work with a few tools to make this happen, but it can be a successful method to finish the hack that you would like to accomplish.

Chapter 19: Secure and Anonymous Using Tor, Proxy Chains, and VPN

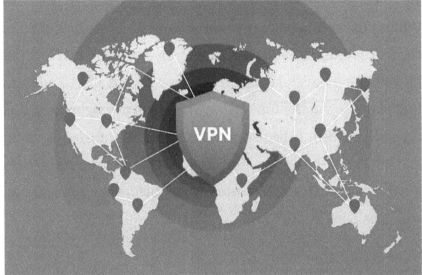

There are going to be some situations where you would like to get onto a network and do some of the work that you want, without other people being able to track where you are going. Being secure and anonymous online is something that a lot of people aim for in their work, and it is sometimes hard to make sure that you can get to this point, and maintain that secrecy. That is why we are going to spend some time looking at the different methods that we are able to use to keep ourselves hidden and safe when we are online.

What is Tor

Tor is going to be a protocol for internet networking that has been designed in order to anonymize the data that is relayed across it. Using this software is going to make it, at a minimum, hard, if not impossible, for snoops to come onto the network and see your social media posts search history, webmail and other online activity that you try to do. They will also find that it is hard to figure out what country you are from, just by analyzing your IP address. This can be useful for a lot of people who want to be online.

When you run this service, some of the bigger data collectors, like Google Ads and other options will not be able to go through and perform some of the traffic analysis that they want, and they will not be able to go through and gather up some data on the habits that you are doing online. This also makes it harder for hackers to gather that information as well.

The Tor network is interesting in that it is going to run through the servers of thousands of volunteers who are found through the world. The data that you use is going to be bundled up in packets that are encrypted when they enter into this network. Then, unlike how we see with our traditional internet connections, Tor is going to be able to strip away part of the header of the packet, which is going to be part of the addressing information that can be used to help us learn some things about the sender, such as the operating system where this message was originally sent from.

Finally, Tor is going to be able to encrypt the rest of the information that we use for addressing, called the packet wrapper. This is something that the regular connections that we use with the internet are not going to use this. Then our data packets, which are encrypted and modified, will be routed through many of these volunteer servers, known as relays, while it makes its way to the final destination. The roundabout way that these packets are going to travel on this network is going to make it harder to track.

Each of the relay parts is going to decrypt just enough of that wrapper to know which relay the data came from in the first place, and which relay it needs to send that packet to the net. The relay is then able to rewrap this in a new wrapper before sending it along again.

While this method is not 100 percent accurate all of the time, it is going to be able to keep your information a lot safer than we will see with regular connections to the internet. The fact that we are encrypting the data that we use, and that we are able to work with this in a manner that relies on relays rather than sending it just one place at a time, can make it a lot easier and more secure to work with.

Using Proxy Chains

Another option that we are able to work with here to ensure that our information is going to stay safe and secure along the way is to work with these proxy chains. These are going to make it a lot harder for the hacker to find us and what we are doing. It will utilize an intermediary machine whose IP address is going to be the one left on the other system, rather than our own. And the Proxy system is set up to make this all work.

The proxy chain is going to be used to help us to accept our own traffic, and then we will forward it on to the target that should receive it. The proxy is going to spend time logging all of the traffic that we would like to send in either direction, but the good news is that if someone would like to look through this log, they would need to get a search warrant or a subpoena to do it, and this makes it harder for us to get onto the other network without anyone finding us.

If we are able to take some of our coding skills and string more than one of these proxies into a chain, it is going to become even more difficult for the other computer to detect the original IP address that we want to work with. On the other hand, if one of the proxies is found to be out of the jurisdiction of the victim, then it is going to be really unlikely that any traffic is going to actually come back to our own IP address.

The good news is that, if you would like to stay hidden with the help of proxies, both BackTrack and Kali with Linux are going to have some good tools that are going to help with doing this process, and this is going to be known as a proxy chain. It is up to you to determine if this is the right option to keep your network secret and hidden.

VPNs

Another tool that we are able to work with when it is time to keep our network safe is the VPN. This is going to stand for a Virtual Private Network, and it is going to allow you a way to create a secure connection to another network through the internet. These can be a great option to use in some cases when we would like to access websites that are restricted based on your region, to help your browsing activity from others seeing it, and more.

These VPNs are really popular though they are not going to be used in many cases for the original purpose for what they were designed for. They were originally made to help connect a business network together over the internet or allow you a way to access a business network when we are at home.

To keep this as simple as possible, the VPN is going to be able to connect your computer, tablet, or smartphone to another computer or another server somewhere on the internet, and you are able to browse the internet with that connection to keep things safe. So, if you see that this server is found in another country, it is going to seem as if you are actually in that company and allows us to pull up information and services that we would normally never be able to gain access to at all.

There are a lot of great ways that we are able to benefit when it comes to working on the VPN. These are going to include:

1. Will help us to bypass some of the restrictions on location when it comes to websites or streaming some of the video and audio that we would like to get ahold of.

2. It can make it easier to stream some of the content that we would like on Hulu and Netflix.

3. Will make it easier to protect yourself from thins like snooping or issues with hotspots of Wi-Fi so that it is harder for a hacker to gain the access that they want.

4. Will help us to gain at least a little bit of anonymity when we are online and can really hide our true location from others.

5. Makes it easier to protecting yourself from being logged when you are torrenting.

It is common for people to work with VPN and other services when they would like to bypass some of the geographic restrictions to watch the shows and movies that they would like in different countries or even to help with torrenting. This can be especially useful when you would like to hack, though, because it makes it harder for others to find you and figure out where all of the attacks are coming from in the first place.

Chapter 20: IP Spoofing

The next topic that we need to spend a bit of time on here is the idea of IP spoofing. This is going to be a process where we are able to create packets for the Internet Protocol that are going to have modified source addresses in them, to either help us hide the identity of the person who is sending the information, to help us to impersonate another system of computers, and sometimes for both. This is often going to be the technique that a hacker is going to use when they would like to perform a DDoS attack against their target device or against the surrounding infrastructure.

Sending and receiving these packets is going to be one of the main methods that these networked computers and devices are going to communicate, and it is going to be kind of the basis of how the modern internet is going to work. All of these IP packets are going to come with a header, which is then going to be followed by the body of the packet, and will contain some of the important information on routing like the source address. In a normal packet, one that the hacker has not messed around with, the source IP address is simply going to be the address of who sent the packet. But if the hacker has been able to spoof the packet, then the address is going to be forged instead.

IP spoofing is going to be analogous to an attacker sending out a package to someone with the wrong address to return listed out. If the person who received the package wants to stop the sender from sending out this package, blocking all of the packages that come from that address is not going to do much good because the return address can be changed as well.

Along the same idea here, if the receiver would like to be able to respond to the return address that they see on the packet, their response package is going to not head to the real sender. Instead, it is going to head to whichever IP address that the hacker stole to use. The ability to spoof the addresses of packets is going to be one of the biggest vulnerabilities that we are going to see with these DDoS attacks.

For example, the DDoS attack is going to be reliant on spoofing with the goal of overwhelming a target with traffic while masking the identity of the source that comes with it. This is going to make it harder to work with any mitigating efforts if the IP address of the source is false, and it is randomized on a continuous basis, blacking the requests that are malicious are going to be a lot harder to do. IP spoofing, as a result, is going to make it really hard for cyber security teams and law enforcement to track down who is causing the attack.

Along the same lines, we are going to find that spoofing is also going to be used to help us masquerade as another device when we would like. So that the responses that come with this are going to be sent over to the device that we are targeting instead of over to us. Some attacks, including the volumetric attacks like DNS amplification, are going to rely on this kind of vulnerability. The ability that we have in order to modify the source IP is going to be a big part of the design that we are going to see with the TCP/IP protocol, which means that we are always going to have to be worried about what is happening here.

Tangential to the DDoS attacks that we talked about before, spoofing is going to be done with the whole aim of hiding and pretending to be another device. This is going to allow the hacker to come in and sidestep the authentication and to gain access to or hijack the session of another user. The hacker is then able to go through the process of doing whatever they would like with this network, which is going to allow them to cause some damage and attack the network, without anyone being able to attach it back to them.

Chapter 21: Penetration Testing with Metasploit

The final thing that we are going to take a look at here is how to work on a penetration test, and how we are able to use the Metasploit system to help us get all of this done. Penetration testing, or a pen test, is going to be a process that involves attacking some of the information systems in a similar way as an attacker would to your system. This helps us to find some of the vulnerabilities in the system and close them up before the hacker can get to them.

The distinguishing characteristic that we are going to find with pen testing is that there will not be any harm done to the system, and the owner of that system will provide the necessary consent before you get started. The vulnerability that we will see will be defined as a weakness in the security that is going to exist in a part of our system that will provide an entry point for the hacker to use to start their attack. There are a number of places where these vulnerabilities are going to show up, such as errors in the design, bugs, and more.

Some of the most common entry points for these attacks and places where we need to check out before a hacker can get to them includes the browsers, SQL injection, flash, ActiveX, and social engineering.

Due to the different scenarios that can cause an attack, different penetration testing types are going to be needed. The three types of testing that we are able to look through can include white box, black box, and gray box testing. When we start out with some of the black box testing, then none of the information about that system is going to be provided back to the person who is doing the testing. It is going to be the responsibility of our tester in order to gather up the right information about the system that they are supposed to attack.

Then we are able to move on to the white box testing. This helps because it is going to provide complete information about the target system from the beginning. This is going to be useful because it helps us to understand some of the impacts that can happen with an internal attack on the network.

And then we finally have the grey box attack. This is going to be where the tester is going to get some of the information about this system, but not all of it. These tests are going to be the most useful to help us better understand what can happen, and the main impact, of one of these external attacks.

So, we need to work through the four stages that are going to happen when we work with penetration testing and the Metasploit process. The first stage that we are going to focus on is the planning out the test that we want to use. The objective of this is to help us to identify the scope and even the strategy that we want to use in order to carry out this test. The scope of this test is going to be informed by currently practiced policies and standards.

The second stage that we are able to work with is going to be known as discovery. There are going to be three things that we are able to do here. The first one is to gather up some of the information on the system and some of the data that it holds. This is going to be known as fingerprinting. Then we reach the second activity and that is known as scanning and even probing system ports. And finally, the third activity is going to help us to identify any vulnerabilities that the system is going to have.

The third stage of this testing is going to be all about the attack. This stage is going to be able to help us identify the exploits for the vulnerabilities. An exploit is going to be a computer program that has the objective of utilizing a vulnerability in order to get the necessary access to that system overall. after the hacker is able to gain this access, the payload is going to be the software that will help them to gain the necessary control over that compromised system. The exploit is going to be done in order to help deliver the payload that we are working with here.

And then we end up with the fourth stage. This is one that can often be forgotten, but if you are doing this process for someone else, then you will want to pay attention to it to help them out. This stage is going to be known as reporting. The objective that we are going to see with this stage is that it helps us to create a detailed report of some of the identified vulnerabilities of the system, the impact that they have on our business, and some of the necessary solutions.

Although there are going to be a ton of different tools that are able to help out with this process, Metasploit is going to be one of the tools that is used the most. That is why we are going to spend some time looking at how to do this kind of process, the process of working with a penetration testing, and how it can be done with Metasploit.

First, we have to realize that Metasploit is going to be a framework that has been organized into modules. The first type is going to be to do the exploit. These types of modules are designed in a manner so that they are able to take advantage of any weaknesses that are found in a system. These are going to be things like code injection, application exploits, and buffer overflow.

Then there are going to be some of the auxiliary modules. These are going to be the ones that will perform some actions, but these actions are not set up to take direct advantage of some of the weaknesses on the system. For example, these can be things like service denial and scanning.

The third type of module that is found on this system is going to be the post-exploitation modules. These are important as well because their main focus is going to be helping us gather information on some of the target systems.

And finally, we are going to find the payload modules. These are going to be the modules that can run after a weakness has been exploited in a successful manner. The payload is going to provide the means to help us control the system that w were able to exploit along the way. With this payload, it is easier to open up the meterpreter to help write out the DLL files.

So now, we need to take a moment to download this system to get it up and running. We are going to go through and do it with the Windows installation here, but you are able to go through and make changes and do some of the work that you would like to prevent other issues along the way as well, and it will work in a similar manner on other systems. You just need to go to the Metasploit website and then click that you want to do the Windows installation.

From here, you will want to download the installer, and then there will be some prompts that show up that will help you to get this installation completed. To help confirm that the installation was a success, you need to start the command prompt, making sure that you are the administrator, and then use the command of "commanmsfvenom.bat -helpd." If you get an output, then this will show you that it worked, and it should list out all of the different options that are available for you to use from this part.

There are a few options that we are able to work with here. For example, if we would like to be able to list out all of the payloads that are available, we would be able to work with the command of "msfvenom.bat -list payloads." This could be a long list, but it still shows us what is available here.

If you would like to go through and start up the console that is available with Metasploit, you will need to use the command of msfconsole.bat. You will then be able to access the msf console, which is going to be the tool that we can use for the command line that is going to work with this program.

The next thing on the list that we are able to focus on, we need to list out all of the exploits that we have available with the help of the command help search. If we want to go through and search around for a specific exploit, you will need to use the CVE number, platform, or name. Let's say that we want to be able to list out all of the exploits that happened in the year of 2018. To do this, we would need to bring out the command of "search cve:2018" and this should list out all of the parts that we need.

To go through this process and then gather up some of the information about the exploit that happened, we need to pass the url of that exploit and make sure that it is in the info command. The code that we are able to work with to make this happen includes:

Exploit/multi/browser/java_jre17_exec.

After we are able to look through the list and then we can find an interesting exploit that we want to use, it is time to use the command that we used above. After we issue the command that we want to work with that specific exploit, it is possible for us to set some of the options that we want to use with the set command. This could be something like setting the local port and local host. The commands that we are able to use to make this one is going to happen will include the following:

set SRVHOST 0.0.0.0
set SRVHOST 8080

If you would like to be able to go through and check the variables that we are able to set, we would want to work with the command, show options to get it done. When the exploit that we are working with has more than one target, we are able to set a specific target by specifying an ID to the set target command. Some of the available targets that we will want to work with are going to be listed with the help of the command of show targets.

Working with the Metasploit program is going to make it a lot easier for us to go through and complete one of our own penetration tests. This is going to make it easier for us to go through and learn a bit more about our system, and figure out where some of the most common vulnerabilities are going to show up and how we are able to close them up and keep the hackers out.

Conclusion

Thank you for making it through to the end of *Hacking with Kali Linux*, let's hope it was informative and able to provide you with all of the tools you need to achieve your goals whatever they may be.

The next step is to get to be where we are able to spend a bit of time learning more about the world of hacking and how we are able to utilize it for some of our own needs. Whether you are looking to protect your own network and make sure that a hacker is not able to get onto the system, or you are more interested in hacking onto another network and taking the information (which, as we discussed, is illegal), you can utilize a lot of the techniques and other methods that are found in this guidebook.

There are a lot of different parts that come together when we are trying to work with hacking, and Kali Linux is going to be a great resource to help us get through some of these hacking, and will ensure that we are able to get this all done. We spent some time taking a look at how to set up the Kali Linux system so that it is ready to go and help us with all of the hacking that we want to do along the way.

In addition to being able to work with the Kali Linux system in order to get some of our hacking done, we also need to spend some time taking a look at some of the other hacking techniques that we are able to use. We are going to spend some time looking at how to do a penetration test, some of the man in the middle attacks, denial of service attacks, how to get onto some of the wireless networks, and the importance of a penetration test.

Then we took some time to look at the different parts that are able to help us to keep our networks safe. For example, with the help of a good firewall and the use of penetration testing, and even VPN's and other options like this to keep your anonymity when you are online, you will be able to make it a bit harder for the hacker to find you, and this makes it so much easier for you to keep all of that information as safe as possible.

There are many parts that come to the world of hacking, and it is important that we learn some of the methods and techniques that come with this in order to keep things organized and to keep the hackers out. When you are ready to learn a bit more about hacking and how it can work for some of our needs, make sure to check out this guidebook to help you to get started.

Finally, if you found this book useful in any way, a review on Amazon is always appreciated!